Hello!

We love Easter! Could there be a greater story to celebrate?

But we also know that when you celebrate the same story every year, ideas to help you do that can soon run dry!

That's where we come in – with this fabulous new resource book. Crammed full of Easter-themed prayer ideas, games, crafts, all-age talks, monologues, and so much more.

All of the ideas contained within this book are brand new, easy to use, tried and tested, and can be easily adapted to suit groups of all ages and contexts.

So, now it's over to you – may God bless you in your ministry!

The Scripture Union Resources Team

welve exciting and easily explained crafts for
ll ages. Some messy, some sticky, some done
uickly, some done slowly – all with a connection
● the Easter story. Within each activity, you will
lso find suggestions for how it could be used
●ithin the context of an all-age service.

CRAFTS

SPONGE PRINTED CANVAS CROSS

Description: an acrylic painted cross using masking tape stencil
Difficulty level: ✱
Bible link: Luke 23:26–49

YOU WILL NEED:

- small canvas
- paper plate
- acrylic paint in two or three colours plus white
- small piece of sponge
- masking tape

INSTRUCTIONS

- Stick masking tape onto the canvas in a cross shape.
- Press down firmly, particularly at the edges.
- Squeeze a small blob of each colour of paint onto a paper plate.
- Use sponge to pick up a little of the paint.
- Dab carefully, but firmly, onto the canvas, so that the colours overlap and form new colours.
- Keep adding colour until the canvas is full.
- Leave to dry, then peel masking tape off to reveal the white cross behind.

Variations:
Try different designs using the tape. Each person could create a letter in the sentence 'He is risen' and then the canvases be placed together for effect.

Easier options:
Use thick card instead of canvas, but test it first to ensure the masking tape doesn't rip the type of card you are using.

ALL AGE EXTRAS:

Create five separate canvases together with the letters 'J-E-S-U-S' on them. Use the letters to talk about Jesus' character. For example: J for Just and Judge, E for Emmanuel, S for Son of God, U for Upright and Unequalled, S for Saviour and Shepherd.

CRAFTS **02**

RISEN, ALIVE, FORGIVEN' BANNERS

Description: a group activity make Easter banners

Difficulty level: ★★★★★

Bible link: Luke 24:36–45

YOU WILL NEED:

- hessian roll, about 14cm wide
- chunky coloured wools in red, orange, yellow, light and dark green, turquoise, light and dark blue, purple
- large-eyed blunt needles
- scissors
- self-adhesive felt in blue, yellow and white
- needle and thread or strong
- tape or staple gun
- hanging rod or dowel

INSTRUCTIONS

- Cut 3 x 60cm strips from hessian.
- On each strip, at top and bottom, make two 3cm folds so that you have a neat edge. Stitch, staple or tape down, creating a loop at the top to hang it with.
- Thread up the wool (allowing about 60cm of each wool) with a needle.
- Knot one end of the wool and then make large stitches through the hessian fabric, creating curvy lines with each colour.
- Use blues and purple on one strip, red, orange and yellow on another, and greens and turquoise on the third strip of fabric.
- Repeat, overlapping the threads, so there are three different colours on each fabric strip.

- Cut out the letters 'R-I-S-E-N' from blue felt; 'A-L-I-V-E' from yellow felt and 'F-O-R-G-I-V-E-N' from white felt.
- Stick the blue letters onto the fabric with blue thread, yellow letters onto the fabric with red and yellow threads, and white letters onto the fabric with green threads.
- Thread the dowel through the loops created by the hem at the top and hang.

Variations:
Use felt or fabric for the back of the banner (though it won't be as easy to stitch through).

Easier options:
Create paper banners.

ALL AGE EXTRAS:
Prepare these ahead of an all-age celebration, and display them on the walls, or fasten individual ones onto the dowel so children can use them in worship.

RESURRECTION COLLAGE

Description: an Easter morning paper collage
Difficulty level: ✱ ✱ ✱
Bible link: Matthew 28:1–10

YOU WILL NEED:
- A5 card
- any used coloured paper in orange, yellow, red, purple, blue and brown, eg coloured pages from glossy magazines, paper wrappings from flowers, chocolate wrappers, etc
- glue stick
- scissors
- silver and purple stick-on jewels
- newspaper

INSTRUCTIONS
- Cut and tear the paper and sort them into different colour groups – orange, yellow, red, purple, blue and brown.
- From the top down, lay them horizontally on the card, beginning with blue, through to purples, then reds and oranges, so that the colours resemble a sunrise.
- Once you are happy with the arrangement, stick the paper down carefully, starting from the top and overlapping slightly as you work down the page.
- Cut a half or quarter circle of brown paper to stick in one corner at the bottom of the page as the tomb.
- Add stick-on silver jewels radiating from the empty tomb.
- Highlight a few parts of the sky by sticking on purple jewels.
- Add the words 'Jesus is risen' cut out from newspaper or magazine letters.

Variations:
- Use fabrics for a different effect.

Easier options:
Use different colours of tissue paper.

ALL AGE EXTRAS:
Create a large collage together at an Easter event that could be displayed for an Easter morning service.

RESURRECTION BAND OR BOOKMARK

Description: a wristband or bookmark made from cord to recall forgiveness of sins

Difficulty level: ✸ ✸

Bible link: Matthew 28:1–10; Isaiah 1:18

YOU WILL NEED:
- about half a metre of white cord
- about half a metre of red cord
- clear nail varnish or PVA glue
- coloured pony beads (optional)

INSTRUCTIONS
- Before starting the activity, seal the end of the cord with clear nail varnish or PVA glue. When dry, knot any ends that will not have beads threaded on them to prevent fraying.
- Explain that the red cord represents the blood Jesus shed for us so that we could be forgiven and made clean. The white cord represents our being forgiven through Jesus' death and resurrection. 'Though your sins are like scarlet, they shall be as white as snow …' (Isaiah 1:18).
- Tie the two cords together in a Japanese crown knot (see photo).
- The knot creates a cross to remind us of the way Jesus died.
- Tie onto wrist to remember what Jesus did for us or use as a book mark.

Variations:
- Leave one red end unknotted and thread with coloured pony beads to tell the Easter story, eg three black beads to represent three days in the tomb, yellow for resurrection, green for palms and the garden of Gethsemane, silver for swords that were used.

Easier options:
- Use chunky wool instead of cord.

ALL AGE EXTRAS:
Use rope to explain that sin can bind us but Jesus sets us free from sin through his death and resurrection.

CRAFTS **05**

PRAYER POCKET

Description: craft foam prayer pocket to encourage children's prayers
Difficulty level: ✻
Bible link: Luke 22:39–46

YOU WILL NEED:
- craft foam
- felt self-adhesive letters 'P-R-A-Y'
- thin strong double-sided tape
- A4 paper or card
- template from page 91
- scissors
- fine marker pen
- pen or pencil

INSTRUCTIONS
- Cut out the pocket from craft foam using the template.
- Stick double-sided tape on to the very edge of the inside of the pocket, then press the two sides firmly together.
- Use a fine marker pen to add 'stitching' around the edge.
- Decorate with felt letters.
- Cut out prayer people by folding A4 paper lengthways. Cut along the fold, then fold into quarters. Use the template to draw around. Cut four people from the paper so that they join at the hands.
- Use each paper person to write a prayer on.

Variations:
- You could cut 12 paper people to represent the disciples in the garden and encourage children to write 12 different situations to pr for at home and school.

Easier options:
Younger children could colour the people they wish t pray for.

ALL AGE EXTRAS:
This could be used at mealtimes to encourage family prayer together.

CRAFTS **06**

PALM SUNDAY TABLE DECORATION

Description: donkey and palm leaf glass jar decoration

Difficulty level: ✱ ✱

Bible link: Matthew 21; Luke 19

YOU WILL NEED:
- 1 x clean jam jar
- 3 x A4 sheets of craft foam in different shades of green
- brown craft foam
- donkey template
- natural garden twine
- scissors

INSTRUCTIONS
- Explain that Jesus had made lots of preparations for this event. He'd sent the disciples ahead of him to untie the donkey he had arranged to ride. Tell the story of the triumphal entry, using pre-cut leaves and donkey to illustrate story.
- Use the template to cut a donkey from brown craft foam.
- Stand the donkey upright in the glass jar.
- Cut 5 to 7 palm-shaped leaves of varying sizes from the green craft foam.
- Snip the leaves diagonally downwards on both sides, ensuring you don't snip through the middle.
- Arrange the leaves in the jar.
- Tie the neck of the jar with twine as a reminder that as Jesus prepared for his journey, we should prepare for Jesus. What could we do to prepare? Pray, read the Bible, be honest, kind...

Variations:
Use fresh leaves for palms.

Easier options:
Use green card for the leaves. Decorate the jar with stickers.

ALL AGE EXTRAS:
You could use these for table decorations for a celebratory Palm Sunday meal or coffee time together.

CRAFTS 07

MARBLED RESURRECTION SUNRISE

Description: marbled paper and collage sunrise to recall the first Easter morning
Difficulty level: ✱✱✱
Bible link: Luke 24:1–12

YOU WILL NEED:

- red, orange and yellow marbling inks
- small skewer or cocktail stick
- aluminium rectangular food tray half to two-thirds filled with water
- A4 black card
- medium white card, cut to smaller sizes than the aluminium tray (paper will take longer to dry out)
- red paper
- orange paper
- glue stick
- scissors
- gold pen
- hole punch
- cord

INSTRUCTIONS

- Spot a few drops of red, orange and yellow marbling inks onto the surface of the water in the food tray.
- Swirl gently with the end of a skewer.
- Place the white card onto the surface and allow the ink to permeate the card.
- Repeat with other pieces of white card, creating different patterns.
- While the card is drying, cut a semi-circle from orange paper and stick it onto a sheet of A4 black card.

- When the marbled card has dried, cut out thin triangles from it, 6 to 9cm in length, for the sun's rays.
- Arrange these on the black card and stick them down.
- Add smaller thin red triangles between the marbled card for effect.
- Add words 'Jesus is risen!' a the top of the sunrise.
- Punch holes in the top and add a hanging cord.

Variations:
Try with different coloured marbling inks, eg greens and blues for a Palm Sunday them

Easier options:
Use pre-cut shapes for the sunrise or simply use an A5 sheet to marble in a larger tra Add an orange semi-circle at the bottom of the paper wher dry and add lines radiating ou from the sun with a felt-tip pe

ALL AGE EXTRAS:

Go large! Have every child create a large marbled triangle (pre-cut to size) as they enter. These coul dry during the first part of service and then be used later to decorate the front of the church.

CRAFTS 08

JESUS IS RISEN' MAGNET

Description: a rainbow fridge magnet made from craft foam
Difficulty level: ✻
Bible link: Matthew 28:1–10; John 3:16

YOU WILL NEED:

- craft foam in rainbow colours and brown
- template from page 92
- scissors
- needle and thread
- double-sided tape (TIP: use a tape dispenser)
- self-adhesive magnet
- pen

INSTRUCTIONS

- From the craft foam, cut out decreasing sized semi-circles for the rainbow shape (see template).
- Cut out the cross from the brown craft foam.
- Thread the needle and use it to make a hole in the top and centre of the cross. Remove the needle and tie a knot in the thread at the back of the cross.
- Secure the other end of the thread onto the front of the red semi-circle with double-sided tape.
- Using double-sided tape, secure the other coloured semi-circles, one by one, onto the rainbow, decreasing in size.

- Write 'Jesus is risen' along the top of the exposed red semi-circle.
- Secure the magnet onto the back of the rainbow.

Variations:
Create different sized rainbows for hanging around the room or for a window display. Use several rainbows in a line for maximum impact!

Easier options:
Use coloured card. A protractor is ideal for a template for the largest-sized semi-circle!

ALL AGE EXTRAS:
Use a larger version of the rainbow and cross, to speak on John 3:16.
The colours of the rainbow could act as a reminder for parts of the verse: red = resurrected/risen, orange = only Son, yellow = you, green = God so loved the world, blue = believes in him, purple = perish not, brown = but have eternal life.

HOSANNA BUNTING

Description: felt bunting to celebrate Palm Sunday
Difficulty level: ✽
Bible link: Matthew 28:1–10, Isaiah 1:18

YOU WILL NEED:
- 3 x A4 pieces of coloured felt in various 'Spring' colours
- 1 x A5 sheet of white or black self-adhesive coloured felt
- 2 metres of 1 to 2cm wide ribbon
- scissors
- thread and needle or staple gun

INSTRUCTIONS
- Explain that 'Hosanna' means 'save us, rescue us'. The crowds shouted 'Hosanna! Blessed is he who comes in the name of the Lord' when Jesus rode into Jerusalem on a donkey. People waved palm leaves, but today we would probably wave flags and hang up bunting.
- Cut seven triangular pieces of bunting from the coloured felt. Arrange them in alternating colours.
- Cut out the letters of 'HOSANNA' from the self-adhesive felt. Stick each letter to a piece of bunting.
- Arrange evenly along the ribbon and staple, sew or machine stitch, ensuring you leave enough room at the ends to hang.

Variations:
Use different praise words or sentences, eg 'Hallelujah! Jesus reigns! Majesty!'

Easier options:
Use coloured card and string or tape to fasten.

ALL AGE EXTRAS:
During the service, using coloured paper or card, ask small groups to create their own praise bunting using different proclamations.

EASY STITCH CROSS

Description: a stitched-cross decoration

Difficulty level: ✱ ✱ ✱

Bible link: Matthew 27:32–55

YOU WILL NEED:

- Plastic canvas
- scissors
- metres of double-knit wool
- tapestry needle with a blunt end

INSTRUCTIONS

- Cut out the canvas cross. To do this, first cut a rectangle 15 holes x 22 holes. Next cut 2 rectangles 5 x 4 holes from the 2 top corners, then 2 rectangles 10 x 4 holes from the 2 bottom corners. Then cut the stepped points and trim the arms of the cross as shown in the example.
- Knot the wool at one end and thread with a needle.
- Starting at the centre with the knot at the back, stitch into the end holes, working diagonally from one end to the other, until all holes are stitched into.
- Now take the wool to the centre and wrap a cross around the centre.
- Take the needle up to the top left hole of the cross, and again work diagonally from top to bottom holes, until all are stitched.
- Take the wool to the centre again and wrap three times to create a diagonal cross in the centre and secure any loose threads.
- Take the needle to the back and slip the needle through the crossed wool to secure the thread.
- Either knot at the back in the centre or take the needle to the top centre hole to create a hanging loop.

Variations:
Why don't you try cutting out your own cross designs from the canvas and use different coloured wools for each?

Easier options:
Use a basic cross shape, and stitch randomly in and out of the plastic canvas for a more eclectic look.

ALL AGE EXTRAS:

- This may be something to use as a reflective prayer activity either at home or in a service. An adult and child could work together to create the cross, while the service leader reads out a series of reflections to ponder on the sacrifice of Jesus for each one of us. Families could take the stitched cross home and hang it somewhere to remind them of the Easter story.
- Create a large version to use in the service, then give out the canvas and lengths of wool so that people can take them home to make and use in family prayer times.

EASTER STORY BOX

Description: Easter story tags in a box to help remember the Easter story
Difficulty Level: ✱ ✱
Bible Link: Luke 22–24

YOU WILL NEED:

- 1 small craft box with lid (about 9cm square)
- patterned craft tape
- scissors
- 12 card luggage tags with printed images on from parts of the Easter story (see page 90)

INSTRUCTIONS

- Decorate the box with patterned craft tape.
- Draw simple drawings from parts of the story onto the tags or use printed drawings to copy and stick onto the labels.
- Use the tags in different ways: ask children to put the images in the right order; see if they can use them to tell a friend the story; take one or two out and see if they can recall which ones are missing. Encourage sharing of the story at home.

Variations:

- Use a small gift bag, plastic tub, craft treasure box or another container to store the tags.
- Use cards instead of tags.
- Use larger tags and a box to use as a group activity.

Easier options:

Use tags or cards fastened with an elastic or loom band.

ALL AGE EXTRAS:

- Use a large version of this with numbered tags hidden around the building, so that children can bring up relevant parts of the story one at a time, to help tell the Easter story to everyone.
- Give each child a box as they enter, then ask them to find all 12 tags (have several of each number at different 'stations'. An adult at each station could tell that part of the Easter story.)
- Extend the activity by having a craft to make at each station.

EASTER PLATE

Description:
Decorating a plate with symbols of the Easter story, reminiscent of a Seder plate
Difficulty Level: ✽

YOU WILL NEED:
- ceramic plate
- ceramic pens or fine point permanent marker pens (though marker pens won't be food safe and won't wash well long term!)
- kitchen roll/wipes
- oven (optional)

INSTRUCTIONS
- Tell the Easter story through simple images drawn onto the plate.
- Draw a simple sunrise in the centre of the plate, to represent the resurrection.
- Use simple images of palm leaves, the cross, bread and wine, dice, crown of thorns, three nails to add around the edge of the plate at intervals.
- Be careful not to smudge the pen while still wet.
- If using ceramic pens, once dry, follow pen manufacturer instructions to bake in an oven to permanently set the colour.

Variations:
- Add more or less images, depending on the ages or abilities of those in the group.
- For older children, you could begin with explaining the Seder meal with a plate as well, drawing simple images of items that would have been used at the Passover meal and explaining their meaning. Egg – new life after a time in Egypt; lamb bone – symbol of sacrifice; bitter herbs – representing their bitter time as slaves in Egypt; parsley – spring herb/new life; unleavened bread – no time to rise before escaping Egypt; salt water – tears of the slaves; *charoset* (a sweet brown mixture made with grape juice, apple, cinnamon, nuts) – symbol of mortar used in the bricks the Jews made as slaves in Egypt.

Easier options:
Use paper plates and felt-tip pens.

ALL AGE EXTRAS:
Create drawings on a large plate in the service, adding to the illustrations on the plate as you explain the Easter story. Use the idea for other topics, eg Passover Seder meal, miracles of Jesus, names of Jesus…

Four fabulous dramas, each highlighting different aspects of the Easter story. Suitable for use within a church service, indoors or outdoors, or as stand-alone features.

THE GREAT EASTER SPRINT-OFF

This drama is all in the actions of the competitors in the race. The only voice is the commentator, who should be heard, but not seen. The costumes can be as complex or as simple as you like – masks or simple pictures that the actors hold would be effective.

CAST

The Easter bunny

A yellow chick

An Easter egg

A hot cross bun

Jesus

A crowd of people to cheer, and then listen to Jesus

SETTING

It's the start of a race to see what the best thing is about Easter. The characters limber up at the start line, with the commentator introducing the different characters. Throughout, they react to what the commentator says.

CRIPT

ommentator: Welcome, dies and gentlemen, to the reat Easter Sprint-off! Today e'll discover who or what the best symbol of Easter. nd without further ado, let e introduce the contestants! lane one, he's got Easter in s furry pocket, it's the Easter unny! In lane two, aw, look ow cute she is; it's a lovely tle chick! In lane three, it's e chocolatey goodness at makes Easter what it is; s an Easter egg! In lane four, ne-a-penny, two-a-penny, it's hot cross bun! And in lane ve, some say he's the reason r Easter; it's the first-century arpenter, Jesus of Nazareth!

There they all are, lining up on the start line, psyching themselves up, getting ready for this make-or-break race. Who will win? The Easter bunny has had a very strong season. Part of the seasonal character training squad, he is coached by Santa Claus and runs regularly with the tooth fairy. The little yellow chick doesn't have very good flat speed, but what she lacks in pace, she makes up for with her face.

The Easter egg sells millions every year, and so he looks confident. His rolling gait makes him ideal for this race. The hot cross bun comes to this event as the queen of Easter baking – she beat a simnel cake in a run-off to qualify for this race. She has come so far; she doesn't want to let things go stale at this late stage.

In lane five, Jesus has fallen from favour in recent years. Not many people even know who he is any more. How will this faded genius fare today?

The starter's ready, the gun's in the air and… *(There is a 'bang' sound effect.)* They're off! The Easter bunny has gone off very quickly and built up a small lead. The Easter egg takes some time to get rolling, but when he does, he takes some stopping. The chick has started well; she's used her cuteness to convince someone to pick her up and carry her to the finish. The hot cross bun has waddled off the start line, but – wait! It's started to rain and her doughy centre is turning to mush!

And what's Jesus doing? He's not running at all! He's turned to talk to the crowd. What a revelation! No one seems to be watching the race any more, they're all listening to Jesus! Where are they all going?

Ow! The Easter bunny has turned to see what's going on and has fallen over! The chick has lost her carrier, who has gone to listen to Jesus. Now the chick is going nowhere! And the egg has rolled completely off course and smashed against that parked car! Remarkable!

The race has opened up for Jesus but he doesn't seem to be interested in winning at all. He's still talking to the crowd. And now they're all leaving with Jesus! Wait! Wait! Doesn't anyone want to see what happens with the race? Which is… er… not actually happening…

Right. Um. Join us next time when we see who proves themselves the greatest Valentine… Oh who cares, I'm going to listen to Jesus. Where did he go?

TEMPLE NEWS

This drama can be cut at several points, enabling you to perform it at different points in Holy Week. You could have it as a recurring theme at different events, or thread it through a single Easter service.

CAST
Huw and Sophie – newsreaders

Laura and Nick – reporters

Benjamin – donkey merchant

Matthew – money lender

Ruth – caterer

Mary – friend of Jesus

Peter – Jesus' disciple

SETTING
Create a 'newsroom' at one side of the front of your space, with a desk and two chairs, or a sofa and coffee table. In another part of your space (it could be the other side of the stage), the reporters should interview the different people from the story.

CRIPT

Section 1: The newsroom is in darkness as some news-style theme music plays. The lights come up to reveal Huw and Sophie.

Huw: Good morning/evening and welcome to Temple News with Huw McDonald and Sophie Bruce.

Sophie: There was a commotion today outside the city gates as Jesus, a carpenter from Nazareth, entered Jerusalem to the shouts and cheers of hundreds of people. As Jesus rode on a donkey, people spread their cloaks on the ground in front of him and waved palm branches in the air.

Huw: Jesus has been travelling round the country telling people about something he calls the kingdom of heaven. Our reporter, Laura, has more on this story.

Laura: Thank you, Huw. I'm with Benjamin, merchant of donkeys…

Benjamin: (Leaning in front of Laura.) The best donkeys in all Jerusalem! Our prices won't be beaten!

Laura: (Pushing Benjamin out of shot before recovering her poise.) Yes OK! Now, Benjamin, you claim that Jesus' friends took one of your donkeys for Jesus to ride on.

Benjamin: That's right! Bold as brass they were! They walked up to my enclosure, untied one of my best colts and said, 'The Lord needs it.' Just like that! Then this Jesus rode the donkey into Jerusalem, with loads of people singing and cheering… It's a wonder my donkey didn't burst an eardrum, the noisy lot. I don't pay my taxes for the Romans to let all my animals be deafened!

Laura: Er, thank you, Benjamin. Huw, back to you.

Huw: Sophie.

Sophie: Huw.

Huw: Sophie.

Sophie: Huw.

Huw: (In a hissed whisper.) It's your turn.

Sophie: Is it? (She stares at her papers.) Oh yes. Sorry. More on this story later. And now the weather. It's going to be sunny. All the time. Huw.

Huw: Sophie. That's all for now. Join us for the next bulletin from Temple News.

The theme music plays again and the lights fade to dark. The two newsreaders shuffle their papers.

Section 2: The newsroom is in darkness as the news-style theme music plays. The lights come up to reveal Sophie and an empty seat.

Sophie: (Shouting angrily off-stage, not realising that she is on air.) Where's Huw? What? Well, he should have gone before we started! (She realises she's on air and recovers herself.) Good morning/evening, welcome to Temple News. Huw. (She looks at the empty seat, then talks to herself.) Well, if Huw can't keep time properly, I suppose I'll have to do his job as well as mine… (Back in 'character'.) Shortly after entering Jerusalem, Jesus went to the Temple and overturned the tables of all money lenders and chased merchants out of the Temple courts. We can go over to Nick at the Temple.

Nick: Thanks Huw… I mean Sophie. I'm here with Matthew, a money lender. Matthew, what exactly happened?

Matthew: He went crazy! He wrecked the place and then chased all the merchants out of the Temple! He just kept shouting that the Temple should be a place of prayer, not a hiding place for robbers. The cheek! I'm not a robber! I've been an honest money lender for many years, and I've never been so insulted.

Nick: (Sarcastically.) An 'honest' money lender?

Matthew: Eh? What are you trying to say? That's typical of the bias shown by Temple News. Come 'ere! (He makes a grab for Nick, getting him in a headlock.)

Nick: (Struggling to speak.) Back to the studio! (Shouting to anyone who'll listen.) Get him off me!

Sophie: Er, thank you, Nick. More on that story in our next bulletin.

(Huw hurries back on set, looking flustered.)

Sophie: (Angrily.) Where have you been?

Huw: (Sitting down.) Sorry, I knew I should never have had that extra-large vanilla mocha latte frappuccino. Now, where are we?

The theme music starts and the lights fade to black.

Section 3: The newsroom is once again dark as the news-style theme music plays. The lights come up on Sophie and Huw.

Huw: Good morning/evening. Our top story: Jesus of Nazareth continues to make waves in the capital. While celebrating the Passover meal, he is reported to have made some unexpected claims. Our reporter, Laura, is on the scene for us. Laura.

Laura: Thanks Huw. I'm here with Ruth, owner of Hebrew Top Brew, caterers to the stars.

Ruth: (Giggling.) Hi Laura! Am I on TV? I've always wanted to be on TV. Hi Mum! (She waves into the 'camera'.) My brother was on TV once, but that was a photofit on Crimewatch. And it looked nothing like him.

Laura: Right… so… back to the story? You supplied some food to Jesus' friends so that they could have the Passover meal, didn't you?

Ruth: Yes, that's right. Best roast lamb in the business! I was just making sure that everything was OK for them when I saw this Jesus bloke take a piece of flatbread, break it in half and share it with everyone. Then he said that it was his body, given for his friends! And blow me down if he didn't do the same with a cup of wine, calling it his blood.

Laura: What do you think that means?

Ruth: No idea, Laura. But the strangest bit was when he said that one of his friends would betray him! I mean, Jesus seems a bit weird, but why would anyone betray their friend?

Laura: Quite. Well, thanks very much Ruth. Back to the studio.

Ruth waves wildly at the 'camera' before Laura pushes her unceremoniously out of the way. Back in the studio, it's obvious that Huw and Sophie aren't ready. They are staring at a smartphone and laughing.

Huw: Look at that little kitten! So cute!

Sophie: *(Realising they are on air and dropping the phone.)* Er, thanks Laura. Huw.

Huw: That's all for now. More on our next bulletin.

The theme music plays again and the lights fade to dark. The two newsreaders start looking and laughing at the phone again.

Section 4: *The newsroom is dark as the news-style theme music plays. The lights come up.*

Huw: Breaking news this evening on Temple News. Jesus of Nazareth, the traveller, teacher and one-time carpenter, has been put to death.

Sophie: Earlier today, Jesus was questioned in front of Governor Pilate, King Herod and a large and hostile crowd. Then he was taken to the place of execution and nailed to a cross. Our reporter Nick is on the scene for us now. Nick, what's going on?

Nick: Thanks, Sophie. Well, Jesus was condemned to death in what seemed like an unfair trial. All the way though, the outcome of the trial was unclear, but in the end, Pilate gave into the demands of the crowd, and sentenced Jesus to death.

Sophie: But what had Jesus done wrong?

Nick: Good question, Sophie. Nothing, it seems. Pilate even said as much during the trial, but the crowd insisted that he be put to death. Now we're getting reports that agents of the religious leaders had encouraged the crowd to shout for the death sentence. I have with me Mary, a friend of Jesus. Mary, can you tell us what happened?

Mary: *(Sadly.)* I can't take it in, Nick. Jesus was arrested last night when one of his friends, Judas, betrayed him to the authorities. We all fled, but his friend Peter followed him. He told me that the crowd shouted for Jesus to be killed. Then today he was… he was… nailed to a cross. Like a criminal…

Nick: *(Putting his hand on Mary's shoulder.)* Thanks for sharing your story, Mary. Sophie, back to the studio.

Sophie: Huw.

Huw: More in our next bulletin.

The theme music plays again and the lights fade to dark.

Section 5: *The newsroom is once again dark as the news-style theme music plays. The lights come up on Sophie and Huw.*

Sophie: You join us as we're getting some breaking news. It seems that Jesus of Nazareth, who was put to death on Friday, has come alive again.

Huw: *(To Sophie.)* What? Are you sure?

Sophie: Yes! That's what it says here. *(She shows him her script.)*

Huw: *(Peering at the script.)* You're right. We'd better get over to Laura, who's in a garden of tombs for us now. Laura, what is going on?

Laura: I'm as confused as you, Huw. I have with me Peter, one of Jesus' friends. Peter, what on earth is going on?

Peter: It's true, Laura, it's true! I can't believe it! Jesus is alive! *(He jumps up and down excitedly, jumping into Laura as he does.)*

Laura: *(Trying to push Peter away.)* Peter! Calm down!

Peter: *(Stopping his jumping.* Sorry, it's just so amazing! Afte Jesus had died, we put him in a tomb. Yesterday was the Sabbath, so we couldn't do anything else, but when some women went back to the tom this morning, they found the stone rolled away and the tom empty!

Laura: Empty? Had someone stolen the body?

Peter: That's what I thought! I went to see for myself and I didn't know what had happened. But then Jesus appeared to us and to some of our friends! I've seen him myself!

Laura: So there you have it, Huw. People think that Jesus is alive!

Huw: Wow! Do you think that' true, Sophie?

Sophie: I don't know what to think, Huw. I think we should find out more.

Huw: So do I. So, viewers, join us for our next bulletin.

The theme music plays again and the lights fade to dark. Sophie and Huw get up and hurry off, chatting.

Sophie: Come on, Huw, we need to find out more about this.

Huw: Right behind you, Sophie!

DRAMAS

03

SOMETHING FOR NOTHING

This drama more obliquely explores some of the themes behind the Easter story, mainly the idea that Jesus calls us to give up something we value (our lives) in return for something even better (a life, and eternity, lived with Jesus).

CAST
Rebekah, Katie, Sophie, Susie, Sarah, Joy – a group of friends

SETTING
There is no distinct setting, so no scenery is needed.

SCRIPT

Rebekah and Katie are looking at a magazine.

Rebekah: Ooh, who's that?
Katie: Oh you know, she was in that thing with that man from the other thing.
Rebekah: *(Sarcastically.)* Thanks, that really clears things up. What's she wearing, anyway?
Katie: That shouldn't matter, Rebekah. You can't judge someone by what they're wearing!
Rebekah: Alright, alright! Keep your hair on. It's just that I saw something like it when I was shopping yesterday. I was only wondering where I could get it.
Katie: Oh. That's alright then. Anyway, how are things with you at the moment?
Rebekah: *(Shrugging.)* It's OK, I suppose. Everything just seems a bit… meh.
Katie: Meh? What does that mean?
Rebekah: It's all a bit dull. I mean, nothing much is wrong – I've got a job that I don't hate, I've got some nice friends…

Katie: *(Bowing slightly.)* You're welcome.
Rebekah: Present company excepted, of course.
Katie: Hey!
Rebekah: Only kidding. I'm just wondering if this is all there is.

Sophie enters, carrying lots of high-quality shopping bags.

Sophie: Hey guys! Look what I got! *(She starts pulling clothes and shoes from her shopping bags.)* These are going to make me look and feel great! *(She holds a dress up to her and poses for the other two.)*
Katie: Oh, that looks gorgeous.
Rebekah: You'll look great in that.
Katie: Hey Rebekah! Maybe we could go to the shops and get you that dress you saw. It might make you feel better.
Sophie: Which dress is that?
Katie: This one, Soph. *(She picks up the magazine to show Sophie.)*
Sophie: Ooh Rebekah, that would really suit you. You should get it. Anyway, what's wrong? Don't you feel very well?
Rebekah: Oh, I don't know. I just don't feel like I'm going anywhere.

Sophie: Well, retail therapy is just what you need. Whenever I'm feeling a bit low, out comes the credit card and away go the blues.
Rebekah: *(Not entirely convinced.)* I suppose so.
Katie: Great, let's go!

The three link arms and start to walk off, but before they can, Susie rushes on, holding a smart phone.

Susie: He's followed me, he's followed me!
Katie: Who's followed you? *(She looks off stage in the direction Susie came from.)* Susie, are you being stalked?
Susie: No! *(She shows the others the phone.)* Olly Timberlake. He's followed me on Instagram!

Sophie screams, Katie looks nonplussed, Rebekah confused.

Sophie: Shut the back door! Oh my goodness, I can't believe you're being followed by Olly!
Susie: I know. *(They both scream and jump up and down.)*
Katie: Oh Susie, get a grip. He probably doesn't even do his own Twitter; it'll be some poor unpaid intern who never gets a day off. They probably just follow everyone back. Give me that. *(She grabs the phone.)* See, he's following 1 million people – it's nothing special.
Sophie: Way to bring her down, Katie. We're trying to cheer Rebekah up, we don't need Susie in a mood as well.
Susie: What's wrong with Rebekah?
Katie: She just feels a bit 'meh'.
Sophie: Nothing a bit of retail therapy won't solve!
Susie: You're on Instagram, aren't you, Rebekah? Why don't you follow some celebs – they might start following you back! Just think, Paloma Ora might be looking at the pictures of your dinner!

Rebekah: I don't know…
Sophie: No, shopping is what we need to do!
(Sarah enters.)
Sarah: Hey guys, what's going on?
Susie: Rebekah's depressed.
Rebekah: I'm not depressed, I just feel a bit down.
Sarah: I know what'll cheer you up – a night on the town. Here, have a look at this. *(She gets out her phone and shows Rebekah some photos.)* See, this was last night's big night. *(She laughs to herself as she scrolls through the photos.)* And I'm up for another one tonight. Especially if my great bud, Rebekah, needs cheering up. *(She puts her arm round Rebekah.)* What do you say? Meet you at 8.30 in the Clown and Coconut?

All the other girls enthusiastically agree, saying 'I'm in!' 'Of course!' etc.

Rebekah: *(Looking doubtful.)* I'm not sure…
Sarah: Oh, come on! It'll do you good! We could take some more photos like these! *(She carries on looking at her phone and laughing. The other girls try to encourage Rebekah. As they do, Joy enters, carrying a bag.)*

Everyone except Rebekah: Joy!

Sophie: Hey Joy! How are you? Ooh, what's in the bag? Have you been shopping too? What've you bought? What've you bought? What've you bought?
Joy: *(Laughing.)* I've got these. *(She pulls an Easter egg out of the bag and shows it to Sophie.)* There's one for each of you. *(She gives an egg to each of the friends. She gives the last one to Rebekah.)*
Sarah: You know what I love about Easter? Extra holidays – with that four-day weekend, you can go out loads!
Sophie: I love it that there are sometimes sales in the shops. And with those extra days off, I can go to that new outlet village!
Susie: *(Showing Rebekah her phone.)* Have you seen Olly Timberlake's Easter Instagram post? He looks so cute wearing those bunny ears!

Rebekah: Yeah… great…
Joy: You alright, Rebekah?
Katie: She says she feels 'meh'.
Susie: She's not depressed, she just feels 'a bit down'. *(She does a quotation mark sign with her fingers.)*
Joy: What's up?
Rebekah: I don't know. I just get the feeling that there's more to life than this. Than shopping, going out, celebrities on social media… *(Sarah, Susie and Sophie start to protest.)*
Joy: You know, Rebekah, I agree. Last Easter I felt all at sea. Nothing I did seemed to cheer me up. Then I was in church *(The others groan at the word 'church'.)* and I started to listen, really listen, to the story of Jesus at Easter. Jesus laid down his life for something better – to repair the relationship between us and God. And he didn't stay dead. He defeated death so that we could live with our God for ever.

Rebekah: Really? I've never thought about it much.
Joy: Yep. He offers this new life freely. All we have to do is follow him. Set aside our old life and have a great new life with him. It won't be easy, but it's better than celebrities, shopping and pints of cider. You want to hear more?
Rebekah: *(Smiling.)* Sure. Why not?

They exit. The others look a bit confused.

Sarah: What's wrong with cider? *(She wanders off, looking at her phone and laughing.)*
Sophie: *(Gathering her shopping.)* Well, I'm going to try these on. I'm going to look fabulous! *(She flounces off.)*
Susie: Aaaaah! Tim Daley has posted a photo of his new puppy! *(She rushes off.)*
Katie: *(Picking up the magazine she was reading at the start and opening it.)* She really does look terrible in that dress. Dear oh dear. *(She exits, shaking her head.)*

DRAMAS **04**

ON GUARD

A drama for Easter Sunday. Try to dress the two soldiers in Roman army uniforms, each with a spear.

CAST
Quintus and Publius –
two Roman soldiers

SETTING
The two soldiers are standing outside Jesus' tomb, guarding it (though they're not sure what from). You don't need to show the tomb, it can all be done through acting and suggestion.

SCRIPT

Two soldiers, Quintus and Publius, are standing outside Jesus' tomb. They have been there a while and are getting a bit bored. They stand side by side, speaking out to the audience, rather than to each other.

Quintus: Quiet tonight, isn't it?

Publius: That it is, Quintus. Just the way I like it.

Quintus: I agree, Publius. When I think of what we could be doing – fighting the Jewish religious zealots or trying to keep peace in the city – this is quite a cushy number.

Publius: Just one thing though.

Quintus: Yeah, what's that?

Publius: Why are we guarding his tomb?

Quintus: What do you mean?

Publius: Well, all it contains is the body of a dead criminal.

Quintus: Mmm. I suppose when you put it like that, it does seem a bit strange.

Publius: Who was this bloke anyway? No one seemed to know back at the barracks.

Quintus: Apparently, he was some kind of Jewish rebel.

Publius: Oh, one of those.

Quintus: Well, that's the funny thing. He wasn't one of those. No one is really sure what he did wrong.

Publius: What? He was put to death and no one is sure why?

Quintus: So it seems.

Publius: Now I know we Romans don't need much of an excuse to put someone to death, but that seems a bit extreme.

Quintus: Don't tell anyone I said this…

Publius: My lips are sealed.

Quintus: *(Glaring at Publius.)* That'll be the day. Anyway, from what I hear, Governor Pilate caved in to pressure from the Jewish religious authorities. They'd made sure that the crowd kept calling for this fella, Jesus he was called, to be put to death. They'd put their spies into the crowd, greased some palms with silver and whipped the people into a frenzy. Pilate thought there was going to be a riot.

Publius: Crickey. That's the last thing we need, a riot. Why were the religious lot so angry with this Jesus?

Quintus: It's hard to tell. Jesus was a religious teacher, just like they were, but his message was different.

Publius: Different? How? Did he believe in Jupiter? Or the divine Julius Caesar?

Quintus: No, nothing like that. You've seen how the Jewish leaders like to make people follow lots of rules. They're always telling people to do this or don't do that, or you can do that but just not on the Sabbath.

Publius: Yeah. If I were Jewish, I think I'd struggle to keep half of those rules.

Quintus: Well, Jesus told people that everyone was welcomed by God, and he forgave people for what they did wrong, so that they could be right with God.

Publius: Well, that doesn't sound too bad. Not bad enough to be nailed to a cross, anyway.

Quintus: That's what I thought, but Maximus – you know him, he's a member of the city garrison…

Publius: Yeah. Big nose, bald head, British accent.

Quintus: That's him. He said that these religious leaders like to keep a strict hold on things, and that Jesus' teaching was threatening their power. He even made fun of them!

Publius: Really? But that's just a bit of satire, isn't it? I love that. You know, the ones we get back in Rome, *Mock the Greek* and *Have I Got Gauls For You*.

Quintus: But he did it again and again and again. Made them look like fools. And the people loved Jesus – thousands of them would follow him around, desperate to hear what he said or to be healed by him.

Publius: He healed people?

Quintus: Apparently. He would heal people *(He snaps his fingers.)* just like that.

Publius: Wow! And it was real?

Quintus: So Maximus says. Said he saw it with his own eyes. But he's from Londinium, so I'm not sure I completely believe him.

Publius: So let me get this clear. This Jesus, who seems like a good bloke, who healed people and tried to free them from all the rules of the religious leaders, gets sentenced to death.

Quintus: Yep.

Publius: And Pilate did it because he was scared there might be a riot.

Quintus: That's one reason.

Publius: So, why are we guarding a dead religious teacher?

Quintus: Everyone's really scared. Pilate doesn't want a riot, it'd make him look bad. The religious leaders think that Jesus' friends might come and steal the body and claim that Jesus has come back to life.

Publius: Are they likely to do that?

Quintus: Don't think so. When Jesus was arrested, they all disappeared. He went from being a leader of thousands to a lonely, broken man.

Publius: Wow. *(He pauses and looks around.)* Nothing's happened so far. Think we're in luck. No riot, no crazy friends of Jesus trying to steal the body. It's going to be dawn soon too. And then we can get back to the garrison and have some breakfast.

Quintus: Ah, that'd be nice. It's been a bit cold standing here all night.

The lights flash and there is a rumbling sound effect. Publius and Quintus do some StarTrek acting, staggering unsteadily back and forth, holding on to each other.

Publius: Quintus! Quintus! What's going on?!

Quintus: I don't know, Publius! Is it an… an… earthquake?

Publius: *(Falling on the floor.)* And lightning?

The noise and lights fade away. Quintus staggers and glances behind him. He gasps.

Quintus: Publius! Look! The stone in front of the tomb – it's rolled away!

Publius: *(Getting up.)* How did that happen?

Quintus: I don't know. No one else has come near us for hours!

Publius: *(Pointing in the direction of the 'tomb'.)* And what's that?

Quintus: It's a light, coming from the tomb!

Publius: Are… are those… people inside? Bright, shining people?

Quintus: This… this is weird… I'm not sticking around here…

Publius: Me neither… out of my way!

The two soldiers rush off, terrified.

These games are designed to fit into your Easter activities. Choose one or more, according to your aims, space, time and resources available. You could stage a family fun day and play all the games in teams, awarding points after each game. Suggestions on how to do this are given at the end of each game description. You could award points to the winning team only or have a scale of points: for example, ten points for the winners, nine for second place, eight for third, etc.

Make sure you risk assess each activity so that everyone is kept as safe as possible.

GAMES

PALM SUNDAY GAMES

STEP ON THE CLOAK

What you need: three cloaks per team (these could be actual cloaks, pieces of material or large sheets of paper), masking tape or chalk

Mark a start line and a finish line on the floor with masking tape or chalk (make them a challenging distance apart!). Split the group into two (or more) teams and line them up behind the start line. Give each team three cloaks and challenge them to make it across the space to the finish line by stepping only on the cloaks. They must move their whole team at once (not go one by one), and one of the team must be on their hands and knees to represent a donkey. If one person steps off the cloaks, they must go back to the beginning. The team that crosses the finish line first is the winner.

If you have already explored the story of Palm Sunday, remind the children of how Jesus entered Jerusalem. To recreate the atmosphere, split the children into more than two teams, but have only two teams playing at a time. The other teams can then stand on the sidelines and cheer for those playing.

Fun day adaptation: either have all the teams play this game at once or play one team against another, and time how long it takes each one to complete the course. After all the teams have played, the quickest team is the winner.

PIN THE TAIL ON THE DONKEY… AND MORE!

What you need: blindfolds (or scarves), a large Palm Sunday scene painted on a length of lining paper (including Jesus riding on a tail-less donkey, a blank space on the ground in front of the donkey and cheering crowds waving their hands), a paper donkey's tail, a paper cloak and a paper palm branch, sticky tack

Stick the Palm Sunday picture onto a wall and put sticky tack on the tail, cloak and palm branch. Gather the players around the picture and challenge everyone to stick the tail on the donkey, the cloak on the empty road and the palm branch in the hand of one of the cheering crowd. If you have already told the story of Palm Sunday, review it now as you look at the picture. If not, explain that this picture will help you understand the story when you hear it.

Blindfold each player in turn and give them the items to stick on the picture one by one, telling them what each item is. The person who sticks the items in the right place (or gets the closest to it) is the winner!

Fun day adaptation: play the game with one volunteer for each team. The player who gets the closest is the winner. If you like, you could award points for the closest for each item, and also for the player who did the best overall.

EASTER TEAM GAMES

EGG BALL

What you need: masking tape or chalk, foam rugby ball, whistle (optional)

Egg ball is dodgeball with a foam rugby ball! Most players will be familiar with the game, but the odd shape of the ball will make bounces more unpredictable and the game a bit trickier! Before the session, set out a court as in the diagram using the masking tape or chalk. Split the group into two teams and position them on either side of the centre line.

When a team has the ball, they should throw it at the opposing team. If they hit an opponent on the legs, then that player has to go to the 'out' zone, behind the opposing team. However, if the opponent catches the ball, then the thrower has to go to their own 'out' zone. Players in the 'out' zone can come back in play if they manage to get hold of the ball and hit an opponent from where they are. If they manage it, they return to their own team's side of the court. The winning team is the one who manages to send all their opponents to the 'out' zone.

You could also play football with a foam rugby ball. You will need to mark out a pitch, as with egg ball, and put a five-a-side net at each end.

Fun day adaptation: play an egg ball tournament. Make a draw and have rounds until you have two finalists. Encourage the other teams to cheer from the sidelines.

OUT ZONE (FOR TEAM A)

TEAM
B

TEAM
A

OUT ZONE (FOR TEAM B)

EASTER EGG RELAYS

Split the group into teams, mark out a start line with tape or chalk and play one or more of these relay races! When everyone has finished, they can eat the chocolate. Watch out for cheating…

EGG ROLL

What you need: one small foil-wrapped chocolate egg per team

Line each team up behind the start line and give each one a chocolate egg. In turn, each player has to roll the egg to the end of the room and back using only their nose. (They will have to get down on hands and knees to do this!)

EMPTY NEST

What you need: a bin filled with hay, bran or shredded paper, chocolate eggs with different coloured foil wrappings

Before the session, mix the eggs into your nest (bin filled with hay, bran or shredded paper). Line the teams up behind the start line. In turn, each player should run to the bin, reach into it and find an egg, before running back to their team. When all the eggs have been found, reveal that each egg has a different value, eg red eggs – two points, blue eggs – five points, purple eggs – eight points. Count up the points total for each team's haul of eggs.

If you have lots of teams, have more than one nest, so that there aren't too many players trying to find eggs at once.

EGG PASS

What you need: large hollow foil-wrapped chocolate eggs (one per team)

Line the teams up across the room. Give each team an egg. Challenge them to pass it from one end of their line to the other. They could do this by passing it over the first person's legs, followed by through the second person's legs, and so on. Or the first could hold the egg between their knees and pass the egg to the second person's knees without using their hands, and so on, down the line. Or the egg could be held under the chin and be passed down the line from chin to chin!

Once the egg reaches the end of the line, the person at the back should run to the front with the egg and start again. When everyone has had a turn at the start of the line, the team has finished the game. The first to do so is the winner.

Fun day adaptation: award points to the winners of each race, but take off points for cheating or unsporting behaviour! You could also take off points for cracked or damaged eggs.

EASTER 'TABLE TOP' GAMES

LOB A CHICKEN

What you need: lots of fluffy little chicks, plastic cups, masking tape or chalk

Mark a throwing line on the floor with tape or chalk. Arrange the cups at different distances from the throwing line and assign each cup with a number of points, according to difficulty. You could have different-size receptacles, such as a waste paper basket, a bucket, a mixing bowl and a pint glass, as well as the plastic cups.

Give each player a set number of fluffy chicks and challenge them to stand behind the throwing line and throw the chicks into the cups. The team with the most points is the winner.

Fun day adaptation: you could play this game with a volunteer representing each team, or encourage the whole team to play and count up all the points. If you have lots of chicks, each team could play all at once, with chicks flying everywhere!

EASTER WORD CHALLENGE

What you need: paper and pens/pencils, letters of the alphabet each written on a small card, an egg timer or stopwatch

Give each player a piece of paper and a pen. Stack the letter cards up and pick four from the top of the pile. The players should write these down on their paper, then, during a strict time limit, they should write down as many words to do with Easter as they can, that start with those letters.

When the time has run out, go through the words. If no one else has thought of a word, then that player gets a point. If someone else has it on their list, it is crossed off and no one gets a point. For contentious words, you will need to come to a group consensus on whether to allow them or not!

If you like, you could draw four more letters and play again. The player with the most points at the end of the game is the winner.

Fun day adaptation: you could play this game with each team coming up with one list of words between them (though this might make a group consensus over borderline words difficult!), or play in small groups, with one representative from each team in each group. The team with the most winners from across the groups is the winner.

EASTER BEETLE

What you need: paper and pens/pencils, dice, sample picture from page 91

Arrange everyone into groups of five or six. Give each group a dice and a copy of the sample picture (taken from Luke's account of Jesus' resurrection). Each player rolls the dice and draws the part of the picture that matches the number of their throw:

1 Angel (2)
2 Woman (3)
3 Peter (1)
4 Joseph of Arimathea (1)
5 Jar of spice (3)
6 Stone (1)

The number in brackets indicates how many of each one the players need to collect. If a player throws a 3, but already has Peter, they do nothing and pass the dice to the next player. Items can be collected in any order apart from the jars of spice – a player needs to have a woman to hold a jar of spice, so has to throw a 2 before a 5. If they throw a 5 without having a woman to hold the jar of spice, they do nothing and pass the dice to the next player. The winner is the first person to complete the picture.

Once everyone has finished, use the picture to tell (or refresh) the story of Jesus' resurrection.

Fun day adaptation: Play with one representative from each team in each small group. The team with the most winners from across the groups is the winner.

STORY OF EASTER BOARD GAME

What you need: game board from page 93, counters and dice

Split all the players into smaller groups. Give each group a game board, a dice and enough counters for everyone to have one each. Each group can play the game at their own pace. The first person to get to the end of the board is the winner. Once everyone has finished, use the game board to tell the Easter story.

Fun day adaptation: play with one representative from each team in each small group. The team with the most winners from across the groups is the winner.

PASS THE EASTER PARCEL

What you need: paper, wrapping paper/ newspaper, a prize, wrapped sweets, sticky tape, scissors, music and the means to play it

Before the session, summarise the Easter story into eight sentences. Write those sentences onto a sheet of paper, cut them into separate strips and mix them up. Create a parcel with eight layers, putting the prize in the middle, and then a wrapped sweet and an Easter sentence in each layer.

Play Pass the Parcel and collect the sentences as you play. At the end of the game, the players should rearrange the sentences into the correct order. Use these sentences to retell the story.

Fun day adaptation: Write the sentences on different coloured paper (one colour per team) and put one sentence from each colour in each layer. The teams collect the sentences as they play. At the end of the game, the teams race to put the sentences in the correct order. The first one to do so is the winner.

GUARDIANS OF ANCORA

What you need: tablets with the *Guardians of Ancora* game app downloaded on each one

Before the session, set up multiple *Guardians of Ancora* accounts on each tablet. (If you don't know how to do this, there is a step-by-step guide on www. guardiansofancora.com.) Show the players how to find the Easter stories on the game app: 'The way to the cross' and 'Jesus is alive'. Challenge the players to complete the Bible Quests. You could play this in smaller groups, with one person playing and others guiding and looking at what everyone is saying. You could swap roles for each chapter.

Fun day adaptation: Keep a note of how many glowing discs each player collects – the one with the most is the winner, and earns points for their team.

EASTER 'HUNTS'

EASTER TREASURE HUNT

What you need: sections of the Bible story printed on cards (see below), clues for your treasure hunt, prizes

Before the session, come up with some clues for a treasure hunt. Your clues should direct teams around your venue in order to uncover the Easter story. So, these clues need to be about the parts of your venue where all the different parts of the story are. You will need eight different locations (though you can have six if you miss out the first two passages). Print out copies of the Bible passages below and place them in your different locations.

1 Palm Sunday – Mark 11:1–11
2 Jesus clears the Temple – Mark 11:15–19
3 The Passover meal – Mark 14:12–26
4 Jesus is arrested – Mark 14:32–52
5 Jesus' trial – Mark 15:1–15
6 Jesus dies – Mark 15:22–41
7 Jesus is buried – Mark 15:42–47
8 Jesus is alive! – Mark 16:1–8

You can also place some wrapped sweets in each location for people to collect as they go round. You can play this in teams or individually. The winner is the first individual or team to complete the hunt.

Fun day adaptation: Play the hunt in teams, with each team setting off after 1-minute intervals so that they can't copy each other. Time each team, with the quickest team winning.

EASTER-EGG HUNT

What you need: lots of Easter eggs of different sizes, a large playing space, a basket or tub for each player

Before the session, hide all the eggs around your playing space. Make some of them obvious and some more difficult to find. Set all the players off hunting for the eggs. Play until all the eggs have been found! If you think some players might find lots of eggs and others struggle to find a few, then limit the number of eggs each player can collect, to ensure everyone gets a fair number. This would make a good final activity in a service/evening/fun day.

Fun day adaptation: You can play this in teams or have this as the finale of the fun day. Convert the teams' scores into time to spend searching for the eggs. The team with the most points get the longest time, while the lowest scoring team has the shortest time. Each team gets to keep and eat the eggs they find. (You might find it diplomatic to keep some eggs in reserve and 'hide' them halfway through the hunt, so that those starting last still have eggs to find!)

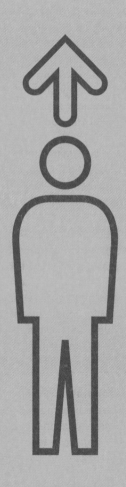

Still or active, quiet or noisy, these prayer activities are designed to help people of all ages to reflect on and pray about every aspect of the Easter story. From the entry into Jerusalem to breakfast on the beach with the risen Christ – these ideas help to bring the whole story to life.

PRAYERS

SEED BOMBING NEW LIFE!

YOU WILL NEED:

sandwich bags, seeds and ingredients/instructions for seed bombs (try www. guerrillagardening.org/ ggseedbombs.html for some ideas)

Explain and introduce the session:
In the Northern hemisphere, Easter coincides with spring, where new flowers are growing and lambs are being born. These are familiar symbols of Easter. Explain that seeds are a symbol of new life and miraculous creation – that in these tiny seeds are the potential for beautiful blooming plants!

As Christians, we believe even more that Easter is a time of celebrating new life! Jesus died and rose again so that we might live and have a fresh start. Jesus explains this to an old religious scholar called Nicodemus in John 3:1–21. Read the passage together. Jesus explains that he is a gift so that we might have a new chance and eternal life – how wonderful!

Use these seeds to make seed bombs! These 'bombs' are a way of planting seeds developed by a movement called 'guerrilla gardening'. They disintegrate and enable the seeds to bloom where they land. Ask the group to think of places in their communities where they would like to see the hope of new life (but encourage them not to be too rogue with where they plant their 'bombs'!). When the group has finished making their seed bombs, pray a prayer of blessing over the 'bombs' – that they would grow and be a sign of new life and hope to the people who see them. Give the group their seed bombs in plastic bags and commission them to take them somewhere they would see regularly. That way they can see if the seeds are growing and can regularly be reminded about the new life and hope that Jesus gives us. Encourage them to pray for the places where they drop their seed bombs. If you do this part of the activity together, be sure to follow your safeguarding policy with regards to trips off site. Alternatively, you can send people home with their bombs and ask them to 'release' them in their own time.

THROWING DOWN BRANCHES AND COATS

YOU WILL NEED:

pieces of paper cut out in the shapes of leaves, a bare branch, sticky tape, pens

Recall the story of Jesus' entry into Jerusalem on a donkey with the group (Mark 11:1–11). Recall that the crowd threw branches down for Jesus' donkey to walk over as he entered in. This was a sign of great honour and showed that the crowd recognised Jesus as a king.

This is quite a dated way of saying that something is important, but what are the modern-day equivalents of throwing cloaks and branches down to say that something is most important and worthy of our utmost awe? Screaming at concerts? Chanting at football matches? Ask the group to discuss what are the most important things in their lives and how they demonstrate this in their actions.

Then ask them to think about ways that we can worship Jesus. What can we do? What can we give him? What ways will demonstrate that even two thousand years later we still believe that he is King and worthy of our worship and praise?

Ask the group to come up with modern-day equivalents of ways we can worship and praise Jesus even when he's not physically there on a donkey! Invite them to write them down on the cut-out leaves and attach them to the branch with sticky tape, and keep coming up with ideas until there is a full branch.

When you're all done, have a go at waving the branch and seeing if it stays together! Pass it round and have fun with it. Finish the session by waving it and praying that we would keep worshipping Jesus as our King throughout Easter and in creative and meaningful ways.

PRAYING FOR THE WORLD

YOU WILL NEED:

world map, one big candle, tea lights, Bibles or printed copies of John 17

Spread out a large world map. Place a big candle on it and light it. Dot unlit tea lights around the map. (Be sure to check this activity for safety, ie make sure your candles don't melt/burn the map.)

Give everyone a Bible (or printed copies of the passage) and ask them to find John 17. Say: This chapter is a look into one of Jesus' final prayers before the cross. It's an insight into an intimate moment in the relationship between God and his Son, and so we see some of the headlines of what's on Jesus' mind as he prepares to die. He prays for his disciples that they would continue to do his work once he has left them.

Either read out the passage yourself, or ask for a volunteer to read it. After the passage is read out, explain: Jesus prays that his disciples, which now includes us, would make God's love known throughout the world. Ask them: 'How do you think we could do this?' Let the group discuss this and come up with ideas. Then ask them: 'Where in the world is there a particular need for God's love to be shown?' Again, let the group share ideas.

Invite the group to pray for the world. Explain that as they pray they can light tea lights from the large candle and place them around the map. The large candle represents Jesus and how he showed us how God loves us, and the tea lights represent us and how we continue to do his work in demonstrating how God loves the world.

Open a time of prayer where individuals can light tea lights and either pray out loud or silently as they do this. (Be sure to warn them to be careful as they lean over candles and to be careful how they hold the tea lights. If you have young children participating in this activity, encourage them to ask an adult to help them place their candle.)

Finish the time by either reading out on behalf of everyone, or having this prayer written down somewhere so that everyone can pray together

Father, thank you that you sent Jesus to show us that you love us. We pray that we would carry out your love to the world and that, through us, the world might see how much you love it. Amen.

EGG PIÑATA!

YOU WILL NEED:

a large balloon, old newspaper, PVA glue, a brush, paints and other things to decorate the piñata with, scissors, sweets, pieces of paper (and something like sticky tape to attach them to the sweets), string, a baton, blindfold

Make an egg-shaped piñata by paper maché-ing a large filled balloon. The thicker the paper maché the harder it will be to break it! Decorate the balloon with paint or crepe paper – get creative! Make a hole to fill it by cutting an opening where the balloon ties.

To make it a creative prayer activity, fill it with sweets, but to every sweet attach a piece of paper/tag that reads 'THANK YOU FOR …'

To hang the piñata, attach some string/ribbon to two holes either side of the opening. Have a think about the baton – I'd recommend a foam bat or rolled up newspaper rather than a wooden bat, for the safety of the group (!) and to increase the challenge of breaking the piñata!

Play the piñata with the group by having a blindfold (eg a scarf) and letting the group members take it in turns to have a swing at it, trying to break it. When the piñata breaks, the sweets will fall out and the group will try and collect as many as possible. (Depending on the maturity of the group, you may want to offer a maximum number they can collect!)

Before you start, explain that this is a piñata with a twist. You've used an egg because that's what we give at Easter, because it is a symbol of new life. Explain that though we remember Jesus' death at Easter which is sad, we also remember it with joy because Jesus said, 'I have come that they may have life, and have it to the full. I am the good shepherd. The good shepherd lays down his life for the sheep' (John 10:10,11, NIV). This helps us understand Easter as a time of celebration and party too, which is why today we are praying with a party game! Explain that each of the sweets has a prayer prompt attached, and for every sweet they pick up, each person will need to think of something they are thankful for.

Once the piñata is broken and all the sweets are gathered, open a time of prayer, where each person takes turns in thanking Jesus for different things.

VINES AND BRANCHES

YOU WILL NEED:

bunches of red grapes in bowls, Bibles or copies of John 15:1–17

Explain to the group that Jesus spent some time trying to prepare the disciples for his death. One of the things he talked about was the metaphor of the vine and the branches. Together, read John 15:1–17.

Have some bunches of red grapes in bowls on the table. Ask them to explain the metaphor by pointing at the different parts of the bunch. What do the branches and the stalks symbolise? What about the vine that we don't see? What do they think the soil that it's planted in is? And what about the fruit? What's the fruit? Is it any more significant that Jesus uses wine made from grapes to symbolise his blood? Allow some time for the group to imagine this passage in reality and extend or play on the metaphor through group reflection.

Ask the group: 'Jesus calls us to remain in his love, but how can we do that? What helps us?' Let the group consider this and come up with some ideas about that.

Explain that now, together, you're going to rest and remain in Jesus' love for a bit, just sitting there in the silence and praying that Jesus would remind them of how much he loves them. Break off the bunches so that everyone has a handful of grapes that they can sit and munch on as they 'remain' and reflect on how much God loves them and how good it is to remain in his love. (Be aware of any allergies in your group.) Pray for the group and encourage a time of silence. You could play background music to help the atmosphere, or songs about how much God loves us.

Finish the time by meditatively re-reading the passage to the group.

MATZO BREAD

YOU WILL NEED:

pieces of paper cut out in the shapes of leaves, a bare branch, sticky tape, pens

Put the matzo bread on plates so that the group can see it. Ask: 'Does anyone know what this is?' Explain that matzo bread (unleavened bread) is eaten by Jewish people to remember the Passover (Exodus 12:17–20). One of the things that this symbolised was the Jewish people being set free from Egypt. They ate unleavened bread because there wasn't time for the bread to rise as they were fleeing (Exodus 12:39).

At the Last Supper, Jesus and his disciples were celebrating the Passover and eating unleavened bread, but Jesus changed what it meant. Something we remember regularly at communion is when Jesus took the bread and said 'Take it; this is my body.' Ask the group what they think he meant by that. Why was Jesus asking the disciples to eat his body? Why do we still do that? Let the group discuss and reflect on the significance of this.

Hand each person their own piece of matzo bread. (Be aware of any allergies in your group.) Ask them to look at the holes and the stripes on it. This is particularly interesting because we can remember that Jesus was pierced by nails and striped by lashings on the cross. In Isaiah, there is a prophecy about Jesus that says this:

'Surely he took up our pain
and bore our suffering,
yet we considered him punished by God,
stricken by him, and afflicted.
But he was pierced for our transgressions,
he was crushed for our iniquities;
the punishment that brought us peace
was on him,
and by his wounds we are healed.'
Isaiah 53:4,5

Interestingly, some translations read 'by his stripes we are healed'.

Give people some time to look at the bread, break it and turn it over. Invite them to eat it and read the whole of Isaiah 53 to them. You could read The Message version to provide the group with a more accessible version.

Then read them Luke 24:13–35. Though Jesus died and his body was broken, he rose again, and appeared to the disciples. Here, on the road to Emmaus, the disciples recognised him again as he broke bread. Finish by praying that Jesus would continue to walk with us and remind us of his death and resurrection in the different moments we break and share bread.

THE JEWISH BETROTHAL CUP

YOU WILL NEED:

glasses, red grape juice

Pour out glasses of red grape juice for everyone. Ask the group: 'What is the significance of red wine for Christians?' Encourage the story of the Last Supper to unfold through the group's explanations and how we celebrate this with red wine. You might read Matthew 26:27–29 to remind them of the red wine at the Last Supper.

Glasses of red wine already had significance and symbolism for Jesus when he invited his disciples to take the cup of red wine and drink it. Ask the group what they might remember about this. It was already significant because of the Passover – the red wine symbolised the blood of the sacrificed lamb that was painted on the Israelite's doors so that the angel of death 'passed over' their households and spared their lives. In this way, Jesus talking about the red wine being 'his blood' suggests that he is like the sacrificed lamb of the Passover.

Glasses of red wine had another significance for the Jewish people of Jesus' day too. It had significance in the Jewish betrothal ceremony too. When a man wanted to marry a woman, he would choose his bride. He would need to settle a price for the bride with her father, before he could enter a contract with her. To seal the contract they would share a cup of wine; the groom would offer it to the bride and if she drank from it, she was accepting the marriage proposal. Then the groom would leave to prepare a room for them to go to when they were married, attached to his father's house. When he was ready, he could return to the bride at any point, and so she had to be ready and waiting.

Either explain to the group the links to Jesus, or tease them out in discussion. Jesus has paid the price for us; he has offered his commitment to us and in our drinking of the cup, we agree to be his. Jesus is preparing a place for us in heaven with his Father where we will live with him for eternity.

Invite the group to take a glass of red grape juice and consider all it means to drink the cup. (Be aware of any allergies in your group, and provide an alternative, if you can.) You could read Matthew 26:27–29 again while they reflect on the story of the Jewish proposal. Invite the group to sip the juice as they reflect and pray, if they would like. After some time meditating, pray out loud to close and invite the group to return their cups.

THE CURTAIN IS TORN

YOU WILL NEED:

Squares of material that is relatively easy to rip, pens that can write on this material

One of the strange things that happened when Jesus died was that the curtain in the Temple was torn in two. Read Matthew 27:45–56. Explain: The Temple curtain ripping at Jesus' death was particularly significant because of what it symbolised. In the Temple the curtain divided the place where people could go into and worship, from the part that was so holy, that sinful people couldn't go in. It was a physical representation of how sin separated us from God. Jesus dying meant that the curtain was torn – we were made clean enough to approach God's awesome holiness because his death has made us 'clean' and holy too.

Even though Jesus' death has made it possible for us to approach God, sometimes we forget that this is possible, or feel 'not good enough' to come to God. Ask the group to think about the things they feel separate them from God. Give each person a square of material and ask them to think about the things that act like a curtain separating them from God's holiness. Give each of them a pen and ask them to write things down on the material.

Once they've had enough time to thoughtfully write these things down, tell them that they're going to rip each other's curtains as a reminder that they can approach God. Ask them to swap with friends and instruct them to take turns in ripping their friends' curtains. Afterwards, read Paul's words from Romans 8:38,39: 'Neither death nor life, neither angels nor demons, neither the present nor the future, nor any powers, neither height nor depth, nor anything else in all creation, will be able to separate [YOU] from the love of God that is in Christ Jesus our Lord.'

MAKING HOLDING CROSSES

YOU WILL NEED:

air dry clay, wipeable work surfaces (possibly a waterproof table cloth!) and some examples of holding crosses

Show the group a holding cross or some pictures of holding crosses. Explain to them:

Holding crosses are small crosses that people can use to hold and meditate over. They are normally made of wood and have very smooth edges. These crosses might be given to people who are in particular need of comfort, or may just be a really useful prayer tool to help us concentrate and pray.

The cross is an important symbol for Christians, especially at Easter. The cross reminds us of Jesus' sacrifice on the cross for us. Therefore it is a symbol of repentance, hope of new life, and God's great love for us.

Give each group member a chunk of clay and ask them to fashion their own holding cross. They could keep it simple or they could use tools (such as sharpened pencils) to add specific words or designs.

Depending on the group, you could either encourage this to be a meditative time, or a time where you just talk. You could discuss how people will use their crosses or where they'll keep them. You could encourage the group to meditatively mould their crosses, while you play some gentle instrumental music, or some worship music that talks about the cross (eg 'Light of the World', 'When I Survey', 'Lord I Lift Your Name on High', 'Thank You for the Cross').

When the group have finished making their crosses (you may need to give them a time limit) prepare somewhere that they can leave them to dry (this will take about 24 hours). You could either give them squares of cardboard to take home, or store them and dry them for the next time you meet.

Once the group have placed their crosses down, pray a prayer of thanks for the cross and ask that these holding crosses would be a blessing in our relationship with Jesus and help us come closer to him.

MYRRH

YOU WILL NEED:

an oil burner, myrrh essential oil, tea light, matches

Set up an oil burner with myrrh oil (available online if there is nowhere local that will sell this). Ask the group about the significance of myrrh in the Bible. They will hopefully remember the myrrh given to Jesus at his birth. Ask them to recall and elaborate on the story. Who gave it to him? Why was it a strange present for a baby? What is myrrh used for? (You can recall the story in Matthew 2.)

If they haven't volunteered it already, ask why myrrh is significant at Easter. Explain that myrrh was used for embalming dead bodies. In John 19:38–42 we read about Jesus' burial and how it was embalmed and wrapped in linen before it was laid to rest in the tomb. (You could read this to the group.)

Myrrh is a significant symbol because Jesus was given it as a baby, and it reminds us that he was sent to die for us. It reminds us of God's outrageous generous gift that he gave us his Son to die so that we don't have to.

Ask the group to pray silently with their eyes closed, smelling the myrrh. Encourage them to let the scent of the myrrh remind them that God had always intended Jesus to die for us. Give them some time to contemplate that and pray quietly as the scent of myrrh fills the room.

You could finish the time of meditation by praying, or by asking the group if they want to, to share anything that they were thinking about.

GRIEF TO JOY!

YOU WILL NEED:

newspapers (it would be a good idea to check for inappropriate content and remove it prior to the activity), bright pens

Introduce the concept of how Jesus exchanges death and grief for new life and celebration. In John 16, Jesus tells the disciples that their grief will turn to joy. Read John 16:16–24. Explain: 'At the cross, Jesus, the Son of God, dying as a man must have felt like the very worst thing that could happen. Despite this, the disciples' grief became joy as death and tragedy became a miracle and a promise of new life. Jesus' reversal of death to new life is a foretaste of the new life Jesus promises us as the result of all he changed by dying on the cross.' In Revelation 21, a 'new heaven and a new earth' is described.

Read Revelation 21:1–7 to the group, or ask someone else to read it. Explain that this is a promise to us, that because of Jesus' resurrection from the dead, God has promised that he will keep turning death into life and grief into celebration until he has finished redeeming us and the world around us. That is what we hope for as Christians.

Explain that you are going to pray for the grief in our world to turn to joy. Ask the group to look through the newspaper and identify stories of grief that they want to pray for. Ask them to take a page and write in bright colours over the story, a prayer that God would turn grief into joy in the situation they are praying for. When they have finished, send your prayers off by folding the pages into paper aeroplanes, as an act of joy! You may want to go outside or fly them out of a window for added drama!

BREAKFAST ON THE BEACH!

YOU WILL NEED:

reakfast food, cutlery, apkins, plates, etc, copies of he breakfast liturgy from age 96

Put out a breakfast spread. (Make sure there is something suitable for everyone – consider any allergies in your group.) You will be limited by time and facilities, but try and make it as posh and celebratory as possible!

Together read John 21:1–14. This is the story of Jesus reappearing to the disciples at Galilee and helping them catch a miraculous hoard of fish. Explain to them that something particularly remarkable and special about this story is that after the tragedy, drama and miracle of the cross, Jesus would do something as ordinary (but wonderful) as eat breakfast with his friends on the beach.

So today, you can eat breakfast together and remember the Son of God who would die for us, rise from the dead, and still come to us and eat breakfast with us in our ordinary humanity. Continue to eat breakfast, but as you do so, say the breakfast liturgy, written here.

Jesus, when we are carrying on
with our ordinary lives
Come and join us for breakfast.

When we are overwhelmed by work
**Interrupt our busyness with your rest
and your peace.**

When we think of you as distant and far from us
**Join us at breakfast, the most casual meal
of our day.**

Come and make your company known to us,
We want to begin each new day with you.

**Jesus, meet us over our egg and soldiers
Or our Weetabix or porridge.
Your presence more precious
Than tea, coffee or our five-a-day!
Help us remember that though we
might be tired,
Our hair and our teeth unbrushed,
You are there with us.
Our companion for each new day.
Jesus, you surprised the disciples
with your company
when they weren't expecting you
and invited them to breakfast on the beach.
Each day, would you pop up in the
unexpected places in our lives.
Would you invite us to sit and eat with you.
Would you change our day
as we remember that you are here with us,
always.**

Amen.

Four fresh and contemporary all-age talks for use as part of an all-age service, a community event celebrating Easter, reflections throughout Holy Week, and more.

ALL-AGE TALKS

52

GOOD FRIDAY

You will need a flip chart, or a large sheet of paper and a thick felt-tip pen. You will also need a piece of string for each person, about 30 centimetres/12 inches long.

Start by asking the congregation to join in a game of 'Hangman' with you on the flip chart, by suggesting letters to fill the gaps. (You don't need to draw a 'hangman'.)

Draw the lines for each letter in advance, to look like this:

_ _ _ _ _ _ _ _ _ _ _ _ _ _ _ _ _ _ _ _ _ _ _ _ _ _ _ _ _.

The correct letters form the following words:

Do what you want and not what I want.

Tell everyone that those words are from Luke 22:42, then ask: 'Who said that?' (Jesus) 'Who was he talking to?' (God)

Point to the completed 'Hangman' phrase. Explain that the words everyone helped to discover are the words that Jesus said to God when he went to pray alone in the Garden of Gethsemane, just before he was crucified.

Say: 'Jesus knew what was going to happen to him. In a few hours' time, he would be nailed to a cross and have the sins of the whole world – that includes us – on his shoulders. By dying in that way, Jesus would be punished instead of us for all those things we do, say and think that hurt other people, and God.

But, because he was completely human, Jesus was in deep anguish and he cried out to his Father, God. Then he said those words we thought about just now (indicate them as you speak) – "Do what you want and not what I want."'

Tell everyone how Jesus knew that, despite the seemingly hopeless circumstances, God was in control and carrying out his perfect plan to save his imperfect people. It was so hard for Jesus to obey God, but he did. And because he did, we can be forgiven for our sins and we can be God's friends for ever and ever! Invite anyone who would like to know more to come and chat to one of the church leaders after the service.

Distribute the pieces of string to everyone and ask them to tie a knot in the middle of their string. When they have done that, challenge them to say to God what Jesus said – 'Do what you want and not what I want.'

As they say it, they should pull their piece of string slowly through their fingers. The idea is that they reach the knot in the string just as they say the word 'not'. It may take a bit of practice!

Suggest that everyone takes their piece of string home to remind them of what Jesus said to God, just before he died on the cross for us, and to be thankful. It can also remind them to pray those words themselves, when they are finding it hard to obey God.

EASTER SUNDAY

Before the service, you will need to get hold of an egg box containing six plastic eggs that open in half (available from supermarkets or craft suppliers at Easter time). Each egg should be numbered with a felt-tip pen or sticker and contain the appropriate symbol, in picture form or as a miniature item:

1 Donkey
(use a toy farm animal)
2 Praying hands
(you could print a copyright free picture from the Internet and reduce it in size)
3 Crown of thorns
(make a miniature one by plaiting modelling clay strips and using the pointed end of cocktails sticks as thorns)
4 Cross
(make a miniature one with two sticks tied together with string or elastic band)
5 A small, round stone
6 Empty!

You will also need the following Bible references, either placed in six Bibles at the appropriate pages, or printed out on separate slips of paper. Give these to confident readers in the congregation who, when they are asked to, during the talk, will stand up and read out the verse they have been given:

1 John 12:14,15
2 Mark 14:35,36
3 Mark 15:16–18
4 Luke 23:32–43
5 Mark 16:1–6
6 Romans 6:9–11

Hold up the egg box and say, 'This is a very special box of eggs. They all have something inside them that helps us to remember what happened at the very first Easter time.'

One at a time and in the right order, invite a child to come forward and open an egg. Ask them to hold up what they have found and explain to everyone what it is, as very few people will be able to see clearly as all the objects or pictures are so small.

There is a simple explanation to accompany each egg's content. Use the Bible verse at the beginning or end of the explanation, and feel free to use your own words if you prefer! Some of the explanations are quite detailed, so use as much (or as little) of the information is appropriate.

1 A donkey: What is this? Does anyone know why the first egg contains a donkey? What happened on the Sunday before Jesus was put on the cross to die? *(You could ask for John 12:14,15 to be read at this point.)* Jesus arrived in Jerusalem riding on a donkey. This was because hundreds of years before it actually took place, one of God's messengers (called a 'prophet') had said this would happen, and now it was coming true!

Everyone cheered and shouted and welcomed Jesus, the King. There were no red carpets in those days, but people spread their coats on the ground and, instead of flags, they waved branches of palm leaves. That's why this day is known as Palm Sunday.

They shouted 'Hosanna!' which is a Hebrew word. It's a bit like shouting 'Hooray', but it actually means, 'Save us now!' Everyone wanted Jesus to save them from the Roman soldiers who were living in their country, but Jesus had come to save them from their sins, although they didn't realise that.

2 Praying hands picture: What do the hands in this picture show? The night before he was crucified, Jesus went to a garden with his friends. He asked them to wait while he went to pray. He talked to his Father God about what was ahead, because he knew what was going to happen to him.

(This would be a good time to read Mark 14:35,36.) What did Jesus ask God to do? But then what did he say to God? He said, 'But do what you want, and not what I want.' I couldn't have done that, could you? Jesus did.

3 Crown of thorns: *(Show everyone the crown and then read Mark 15:16–18.)* Basically, the soldiers bullied Jesus. That's horrible. They were making fun of him when they pushed that crown down onto his head. How it must have hurt! But the soldiers didn't realise when they gave him a pretend crown, that Jesus really was the King of kings!

4 A cross: This cross reminds us of the real, rough wooden cross that Jesus was nailed to. *(You could invite the reader to read Luke 23:32–43 now.)* Even when he was being crucified, Jesus was still able to ask God to forgive the people who were killing him!

Jesus let all that horrible stuff happen to him because he knew that it was the only way that God could forgive the whole world – including us – by letting him take the punishment that they (and we) deserved.

5 A stone: What was the first thing that the women saw when they went to put spices on Jesus' body? Yes, the stone had been rolled away and the tomb was empty. *(This would be a good time to ask for Mark 16:1–6 to be read.)*

Jesus was alive! It was amazing! Jesus is alive! It is amazing! Not only did God show his power over sin when Jesus died on the cross, he also showed his power over death when he came back to life! That's what we are celebrating today (and that's one of the reasons why we have Easter eggs – to remind us of the empty tomb and also of the new life God gives.)

6 An empty egg: What's inside? Nothing! This final egg is empty to remind us that Jesus isn't dead, he's alive! He wants us to ask for forgiveness so that we can be friends with God and live with him for ever, starting now, and one day in the future, in heaven… for ever and ever and ever! *(Finish by asking for Romans 6:9–11 to be read to everyone.)*

T-SHIRTS

ROMANS 5:8

INTRODUCTION

This talk uses simple language and visual imagery to convey meaning. Often 'seeing' what Jesus did helps us to know and understand it in our head and our hearts. This talk could be used effectively at a Good Friday service (in church, or on a walk of witness), or as part of an Easter Sunday service.

YOU WILL NEED

- two new white T-shirts
- black paint (not too wet) or a large black marker pen
- two volunteers primed in advance (both wearing old tops underneath their white T-shirt in case the paint or marker pen soaks through, and thus making the exchange during the talk a little easier)

TALK

To begin, show the following 'slide to go' clip from YouTube https://www.youtube.com/watch?v=X2cs8gnb42A or come in with a stain on your own shirt. Invite your two volunteers to stand at the front of the church with their backs to the congregation, wearing the white T-shirts.

A script for the talk is provided below. You can either use the script as it is, or adapt it to work best with your congregation.

Having a stain is irritating, isn't it? I am sure that, at some point, you have put on a new top and straight away you get ketchup right down the front. It's always in an obvious place! Maybe it doesn't start talking, but it feels like it does. It's like everyone is looking at it. Everyone can see it.

We are going to think about the stains, not on our clothes, but those in our lives. Some we can see, some we can't. They are the kind that, no matter how hard we try, we can't get rid of – at least, not by ourselves. At this time of year we remember how those deep stains can be removed – for ever.
Every day we do things that God wouldn't want, don't we? It's something that the Bible calls sin. It's just a **little word** but it has caused **big** problems. Put simply, sin means doing wrong things, things that God wouldn't want. I know we might try to do good things, but sadly we more often do wrong things. I know I do.

What are the sorts of things we do that are wrong? Any ideas? *(Encourage people to call out their ideas. If there is a lack of response, prompt them with some of your own suggestions.)* So let me start – sometimes I get angry… anyone else? Perhaps we might lie, cheat, behave selfishly, think bad thoughts, do nasty things, or even steal and hate. *(As each idea is suggested, write it on one of the white T-shirts or simply make dark marks.)*

Now, that is looking quite a mess. It was a lovely clean white T-shirt – until I messed it up. Once we were all lovely and white and clean, like this T-shirt *(point towards the volunteer wearing the clean T-shirt)*, but, well, you can see what our sin has done *(point at the volunteer with the dirty T-shirt)*. All these things make us really dirty. We are all covered with these stains. They are not the kind of stains that we can wash off ourselves – they aren't just on the surface, they go right through us. This is the biggest problem of all because it's our own bad stuff, **it's our sin**, that blocks us from having a friendship with God.

So… we are in big trouble. We can't clean ourselves. So what are we going to do? We need help – someone to sort it all out. We just aren't strong enough and if we can't get clean, we'll face the results of sin: sadness in this life and an eternity without God.

This is what Jesus did on the cross for us.

(At this point, ask the volunteers to exchange their white T-shirts. The one who ends up with the dirty one should now stand with their arms outstretched – like Jesus on the cross.)

Paul wrote this in Romans 5:8: 'But God demonstrates his own love for us in this: while we were still sinners, Christ died for us.'

It was as though Jesus, who was perfect and spotless – like the clean T-shirt – swapped T-shirts with us. He wore our dirty one. He did this while we didn't even care. He took our sin and nastiness once and for all because he loves us and wants to save us from sin's consequences.

And because he died and came back to life, he can give anyone who asks him a clean T-shirt – a clean and new life – a fresh start. It's as if those who believe in Jesus now wear his white T-shirt. It doesn't mean we are perfect – far from it. It means that we recognise that we aren't. Because it's his T-shirt, not ours, that we wear!

Each one of us needs to give him our dirty T-shirt. We need to ask him to take away our own sins and destroy them for ever, so we can live, serve and follow him for eternity.

'But God (shows us) his own love for us in this: While we were still sinners, Christ died for us.'

TORN CURTAIN

MARK 15:33–41

INTRODUCTION

This talk would be ideal for an Easter Sunday service. In advance, set up a large curtain across the main area where you lead worship, allowing a space in front of it so your service can carry on until the talk. You may need to secure some rope or strong twine across the room to hang the curtain on. Depending on the curtain material you use (not too heavy but not too transparent either), it may need a further support in the middle so it doesn't hang down too much. Hopefully, as people arrive and see the large curtain across your church, it will provoke interest and conversation. During the talk you will cut the string or pull the curtain down. If you have communion on Easter morning, it might be good for people to walk through where the curtain was hanging to receive their bread and wine.

YOU WILL NEED

- two dark curtains
- rope or strong twine
- garden clippers or other strong cutting tool
- image of Temple from page 94

TALK

...script for the talk is provided ...elow. You can either use the ...cript as it is, or adapt it to work ...est with your congregation.

...he curtain may have surprised ...ou today. Perhaps you like ...oking at the windows *(or ...hatever has been covered ... the curtain)*. Or perhaps, for ...ome, it's the empty cross *(if ...ou have one)* you like to see.

...ut imagine if this was here ...very week. You might wonder ...hat's behind it – I certainly ...ould. Our curtain, our veil, ...uts that off from you, doesn't ...? Do you want to know what ... who is behind it? I know I do!

... Jesus' day in Jerusalem, ...was always like that in the ...emple. In fact, we wouldn't be ...lowed in this bit of the church ...it were the Temple, as we are ...entiles (that's everyone who ...n't Jewish). We would all be ...utside the church building ...together.

...ere's a picture of the Temple ...s Jesus would've seen it. *...isplay the image, or ...escribe it.)*

The outer courts are for Gentiles, that's you and me. Beyond that is the main part of the Temple, and then, on the other side of a curtain, is the Holy of Holies. Its size, colour and patterns are described in the book of Exodus in the Old Testament. It was absolutely amazing – a gold room in the shape of a cube.

The Temple had layers, a bit like an onion – the more layers you went through, the closer you would get to the place where God lived. People believed that if you walked in the Temple you were on the edge of the place God lives. Even though they knew he was bigger than that, over the years they had come to believe that God actually lived in the Temple. It was where they believed they could meet him. Well, at least a priest could meet him there, once a year! God was there and he was too holy, too awesome, too great, too magnificent for people like you and me. The priest could go in, but only after days of preparing and washing. And even then he was only allowed in once a year on the Day of Atonement. Some traditions say that a rope was tied to the priest's ankles, just in case he died and needed to be pulled out. Since no one else was allowed inside, that would be the only way to get him out!

That curtain in the Temple was there all through Jesus' life. It separated the Holy of Holies from the rest of the Temple. From Jesus' birth to the years he spent healing people, feeding 5,000, stilling a storm, entering Jerusalem and finally being falsely arrested and nailed to a cross – through all of that, the curtain in the Temple was there. And it's after Jesus was nailed to the cross that we meet the curtain again.

With a loud cry from the cross, Jesus died. As Jesus took his last breath on the cross, the curtain that had been there for hundreds of years, extra large and super heavy, was ripped from top to bottom. The curtain tore at the very moment Jesus died. This is really, really important.

Jesus died to deal with all our bad stuff, all the sins that we have ever committed and will ever commit. Our sins are a bit like a wall of wrong that separates us from God's presence. Our sins are a bit like the curtain in the Temple. They keep us separated from God.

Believing in and accepting Jesus makes a way for us to enter the holy of holies, and meet God himself. Not in a temple but in our own hearts. Jesus' one-time act upon the cross rips open the way into the presence of God. Even though we could never be good enough to enter the holy of holies on our own, Jesus makes it possible.

'Therefore, brothers and sisters, since we have confidence to enter the Most Holy Place by the blood of Jesus, by a new and living way opened for us through the curtain, that is, his body, and since we have a great priest over the house of God, let us draw near to God with a sincere heart and with the full assurance that faith brings …' (Hebrews 10:19–22a)

(While reading this, pull down the curtain. You could cut the wire/twine yourself, or invite some children to help you pull it down – as long as this is safe!)

Jesus doesn't just pull back the curtain to show us the other side. He tears the curtain completely open, by his death on the cross. You see, God hasn't changed. But, through Jesus, we are being changed. God is no less awesome, he is no less holy, but now, through Jesus, we can enter into his presence. We can meet him for ourselves, and he can live in our hearts – always with us.

We simply need to step through and meet him.
(Step through/over the curtain with the children.)

Sometimes it's helpful to think about the Easter story from a new perspective. What might the disciples have been thinking and feeling? What would it have been like to be Mary Magdalene discovering the empty tomb?

MONOLOGUES

THE LAST SUPPER

Bible reference:
Matthew 26:17–35

Themes: Wondering,
Questioning, Confusion,
Uncertainty, Importance,
Betrayal, Denial

Presentation style: Either
as a reflective reading or as a
person 'in character' on 'stage'.

**This monologue is written from the
perspective of one of the disciples who
asked Jesus where they ought to prepare
the Passover meal. The monologue
proceeds from this point in the story,
until Jesus and his followers depart to
Gethsemane.**

knew it was coming up to that time when we needed to get everything ready for the Passover meal. But Jesus adn't said anything about where we were going to elebrate. We'd been on the ad for a while, and I kept ondering when we'd stop. My eet were so achy and tired.

the end, we just decided to sk him, and see what he said.

e told us to go ahead into the ity nearby and find a man. He dn't say how we'd know it as the right man, but I didn't are ask. I hoped it would all ecome clear. So we went into wn, and do you know what? couldn't have been clearer. omehow we just found the ght man and told him that sus, the Teacher, had chosen s house to celebrate the assover meal.

be honest, I was a bit orried about what he ight say – but he seemed solutely fine. So we went side and got everything ady. There would be 13 of us ere that night, remembering w our ancient ancestors had scaped from Egypt, how God as rescued them from slavery.

Eventually everyone else arrived and we started to eat. Tired feet resting, tasty food in our bellies and remembering a wonderful God who saved us. The house was perfect; there was just enough room for all of us there, and we were happy. But not for long.

Completely out of the blue, Jesus said, 'Tonight, one of you is going to turn on me. One of you is going to betray me.' Everyone stopped, stared, food halfway to our mouths… We must have heard him wrong, surely. Our faces said it all, 'Come on Jesus, tell us we misheard you?' but he didn't say anything. I looked around the table at everyone else. Fear, shock, total disbelief was on everyone's faces. Betray Jesus? Never. No way. Not happening. How could he even think that anyone could?

All at once everyone started talking. 'It's not me, Lord', 'I'd never betray you', 'No way!' 'Is it me? It can't be!'

Then Jesus spoke again. He said that whoever it was would wish they'd never been born. Silence fell on the room again. I could feel the tears welling up in my eyes. Surely this wasn't happening. It couldn't be.

Then Judas whispered, 'Is it me?'

Our heads slowly turned to face Judas. He suddenly looked guilty, ashamed, almost like he wanted to hide.

'Yes, it's you,' Jesus said.

I wanted to kill him. I wanted him gone. How could he even think of doing such a thing? I never trusted him; he always had a sneaky look in his eye. I decided it was time for him to leave.

But before I could do anything, Jesus held up some bread, above his head. He was looking straight up at it, or past it maybe, and saying something else I'd never have expected.

'This bread is my body. Take it and eat it.' Then he passed it round and we all ate some in silence.

Then he lifted up a cup of wine, only this time he said, 'This is my blood, all of you drink it.' So we did.

(long pause)

I didn't know what to think anymore. Everything I thought I knew about Jesus I questioned. He kept saying he was going to die, he was going to leave us, but how? Why? I haven't even known him that long. He's young, healthy; he's a wonderful teacher and I've seen him do truly incredible things. He can't just die. Can he?

As if he knew what I was thinking, Jesus started saying that we would all stumble in our faith. That we'd have questions, and not know what we believed any more, just because of the things that were going to happen to him.

But Peter said he wouldn't. Peter said he'd never lose his faith. He'd always stay strong and follow Jesus for ever. But Jesus told him that even now, even on that day he'd lose his faith. He told Peter that he'd deny he even knew Jesus, not once, but three times! How did he know?

Peter was adamant. There was no way he'd ever do that. Not three times, not even once. He even said he'd follow Jesus to his death, and that he'd die for him. But Jesus kept on saying that wasn't true, and that all of us, every single one of us would desert him.

The feeling in the room wasn't so happy anymore. No one felt rested. No one wanted to eat or celebrate. Everyone was sad and angry and confused and afraid.

Jesus left the room. 'I'm going to pray,' he said. We trailed out after him, wondering where we were going as we walked off into the darkness. I couldn't think straight, I didn't know what to do. Was there anything I could have done? Should have done?

Surely, surely, he's not going to die?

MONOLOGUES **02**

AT THE CROSS

Bible reference:
Luke 23:26–47

Themes: Crucifixion, Death, Sacrifice, Atonement, Heaven, Sadness, Injustice, God's plan

Presentation style: Either as a reflective reading or as a person 'in character' on 'stage'.

This monologue is written from the perspective of the army officer who witnessed the crucifixion of Jesus and, upon seeing what happened, realised that a great injustice had taken place. He is recorded in Luke's Gospel as saying 'Surely this was a righteous man!' (v 47, NIV) after Jesus had died.

know it's grim, but I've seen enough crucifixions to last me lifetime. It's a hideous way to e. I'm not proud that I've been part of it. But it's what we o – to the bad people I mean. hat's how we punish them, ow we make sure everyone ealises breaking the law has erious consequences.

sually, they're the worst of e worst. Criminals that have one terrible things. But this ne, something was different. t least with one of them nyway.

he guy in the middle. He was fferent. He brought a massive owd with him too. Normally eople do come up here and atch – I don't know why, but ey do. But today, there were ay more than usual.

ut even before they brought m here, he was causing aos. Pilate didn't think e'd done anything wrong, ut everyone wanted him ead. They said he was a oublemaker. They said he ept saying things, making out at he was the Messiah.

Everyone says he's done amazing things. I've heard that he's healed sick people, he's fed thousands with a just a few fish and loaves of bread, he can make storms stop and turn water into wine. That's what they said. Why would you want to kill a man who can do amazing things like that?

Anyway, they made him carry his own cross all the way up here. Except he kept falling. They'd beaten him up pretty bad and made him wear this ridiculous purple robe. They'd even made him this horrible crown, out of thorns, and pushed it onto his head. Eventually, some other guy, Simon, I think his name was, ended up carrying the cross instead.

His name was Jesus – the man they wanted dead, the miracle worker and teacher.

They hung him there, on the cross, with two thieves. He was in the middle; they were on his left and right.

People didn't usually say much when they were hanging there. I'd imagine the pain was far too much for them to think about speaking. But Jesus did.

'Father, forgive them, they don't know what they're doing,' he said.

I wasn't sure what he meant, but asking for forgiveness for people who were punishing him, that's an incredible thing to do. Especially since he didn't deserve any of the punishment in the first place.

The other officers hanging around started playing a game. I mean it was hardly a good time, but they decided to roll dice and see who got the highest score. The person who won, got some of Jesus' clothes. They asked me to join in, but I couldn't.

People kept shouting at Jesus, making fun of him. 'If you're the one you say you are, come on down and save yourself', 'I thought you were the chosen one', 'Not so special now are you?' – all kinds of horrible things. But he said nothing. They even stuck a sign on the cross above his head that said 'King of the Jews' and they pointed at it and laughed.

Even the thieves joined in, shouting at him from their crosses, but only one told him to save himself, the other said something odd. He yelled all the way across to the other thief and told him to stop.

'Don't you see? You're here because you deserve to be, but this man isn't. He hasn't done anything wrong. You should be afraid.'

Then he spoke to Jesus directly and said, 'Jesus, remember me today when you come into your kingdom.' And Jesus replied. 'Today, I tell you, you will be with me in paradise.'

Wow. Just wow. The more I looked at Jesus, the more I realised how special he was. This was all wrong; it didn't make sense. He seemed to be there willingly; he seemed to know what was happening to him all along, and even though he didn't want it to happen, it seemed as if he did.

Not long after that, Jesus died. When he took his last breath everything suddenly went really dark, like a dark night without a moon, and there was an enormous earthquake. Everyone screamed and people ran all over the place; no one knew what was going on. It was so, so scary.

I knew he was a good man. I knew it. I said out loud, to anyone who would listen, 'Surely this was a good man!'

MARY MAGDALENE

Bible reference:
John 20:1–16

Themes: Resurrection,
Surprise, Amazement, Joy,
Angels, Hope

Presentation style: Either
as a reflective reading or as a
person 'in character' on 'stage'.

**This monologue is written from the
perspective of Mary Magdalene after she
has visited the empty tomb and encountered
Jesus. Mary is one of the first people to see
the risen Christ, and she is overwhelmed
with emotion.**

I went there this morning. I had to see him again. Or at least, I had to see where they laid him.

The last three days have been the worst and best days of my life. I've never been so sad, and I've never been so happy. I've never been so scared, and I've never been so amazed. I've never been so afraid of the future and I've never had so much hope.

Let me explain.

My Lord, Jesus, they crucified him. They nailed him to a cross and left him there until he died. He didn't deserve it, he did nothing wrong, but they wanted him gone. That was three days ago.

They wrapped him in cloths and put him in a brand new tomb – they tried their best to give him a good burial. Then they rolled an enormous stone across the entrance of the tomb and left him there.

Then it was the Sabbath day. I couldn't go to visit the tomb, I couldn't get near to him. It wasn't allowed. I spent the day crying; the tears just wouldn't stop. I couldn't believe he was really gone.

So early this morning, I ran to the tomb. I wanted to sit there and just be near him. I ran as fast as I possibly could, but what I saw, I could never have imagined. The stone, that enormous great big stone that took so many men to move, it had been rolled away. I could see right inside.

I almost daren't look. I couldn't bring myself to see him lying there, but I did look. And he wasn't. He wasn't there at all! The clothes they wrapped him in were there, but his body was gone. I didn't know what to do. So I ran back and found Simon Peter, and between my gasping for breath and tearful sobs I managed to tell him what I'd seen.

Peter followed me back there. He ran ahead and got there first – I didn't have the energy left to keep up with him! He went inside and came out again straight away. Everything was just how it was when I'd left a few moments before. Peter didn't know what to do either! So he went back to tell the others that he'd seen just what I'd seen.

I waited. I needed to sit down after all that running back and forth. I thought I'd just take one more look inside the tomb before I sat down for a rest. But as I stood there, looking inside, the tears came back and ran down my face like a river. When I looked up again I nearly fainted. Right there, in the tomb, there were two men.

Well, I think they were men – they were white and glowing and incredibly bright. One sat where Jesus' head had been and the other where his feet had been. They looked at me and asked me why I was crying.

Why am I crying? How could I explain? I told them that my Lord had been taken away and I didn't know where they'd taken him.

I turned around and there was another man, just standing there. He asked me why I was crying, too. I looked around to see where the other two men had gone, but I couldn't find them. 'Who are you looking for?' this new man said.

I thought it must be him. He must've moved Jesus. He looked like a gardener, and maybe he'd seen where someone else had taken the body. I tried to explain, and I asked him where Jesus had gone. Then, he said my name. I hadn't told him my name, but he knew it.

Mary.

At that very moment I saw him. It was my Lord. Jesus. He was standing there, right in front of me. Alive and radiant. He wasn't dead, his body wasn't in the tomb. He wasn't there, because he was alive! And he still is! Jesus is alive!

MONOLOGUES

04

A FISHY BREAKFAST

Bible reference:
John 21:1–14

Themes: Resurrection, Hope, Joy, Miracles, Jesus, Breakfast, Fishing

Presentation style: Either as a reflective reading or as a person 'in character' on 'stage'.

This monologue is written from the perspective of Simon Peter, after he and several other disciples decide to go fishing. They encounter Jesus, failing to recognise him at first, but end up enjoying a wonderful breakfast with him on the beach.

ove fishing. It's all I've ever
nown. Out on the water,
sting in the boat, pulling up
e nets, fish, fish, and
ore fish.

specially in the morning,
at's the best time.
ometimes I go in the evening
o, but I'll never catch as
any. In fact, last night I didn't
tch anything. I mean, it's not
ecause I'm a bad fisherman
honestly, it's not – there just
eren't any fish!

anyway, we went out again
is morning. Surely we'd catch
me this time. But weirdly,
ere still didn't seem to be any
h. Everywhere we tried, our
ts came up empty.

ter a while, I noticed a man
anding on the shore. Every
ne I looked over there I could
e he was watching us. As
got a bit closer to him he
outed, 'My friends, have you
ught anything?'

I don't really know why he
asked, because he could see
that our nets were empty, and
he'd been there for quite a
while, so he knew we'd been
trying for ages. I told him we
hadn't even caught a tiddler.
But then he said, 'Throw your
nets over the right side of the
boat, you'll find some
fish there!'

I mean, how did he know where
the fish were? I'd been looking
all morning!

Anyway, we dropped the nets,
not really sure if there would be
any fish when we pulled them
up, but then when we tried,
we couldn't pull them back in.
There were so, so, so, so, so,
so, so many fish!

Then we realised. It was the
Lord! My Lord, he was here!
Right there on the shore. I
couldn't wait to see him. I had
to get to him as quickly as I
could. So I jumped out of the
boat (with my coat on – don't
know why I did that, but never
mind!) and tried to run through
the water to Jesus.

Have you ever tried to run in
water? It didn't go so well. I
splashed around a lot, got very,
very wet, but I made it to the
beach eventually. Everyone
else was just behind me,
dragging in the boat and the
fish – but I got there a couple
of seconds before them, so
it was definitely worth a
soggy coat!

Like I said, I like fishing, it's my
thing. I also like eating fish,
and I especially like the smell
of them cooking. And weirdly,
that's exactly what I could
smell right then. I looked at
Jesus, then I looked down by
his feet, and there was a fire of
hot coals with wonderful fresh
fish cooking away, a big loaf of
bread for us all to share – and I
suddenly realised how hungry
I was!

Jesus told me to go and get
some of the fish we'd just
caught and bring them over.
There were so, so many! (I
counted them that afternoon,
there were 153, can you
believe it?!) Anyway, I pulled
the net further up the beach
and grabbed a few fish to add
to the fire.

We all sat down with Jesus and
he passed around the bread
and the fish. I'll never forget my
breakfast with Jesus – it was
the best breakfast I've
ever had!

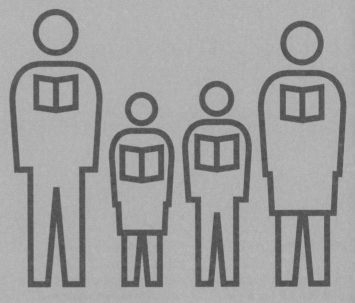

Have you ever wondered how you might use seven different colours to retell the Easter story? Keep reading to find out!

ALL-AGE SERVICE

COLOURFUL EASTER

Things you will need:
colourful coated chocolates, eg Smarties; Easter poem from page 96 to give out; fabric pieces, flags or large card segments (eighths) in green, orange, purple, red, brown, blue, yellow and pink; or have images on screen of segments added to a circle one by one, in colour order of talk.

1

TRODUCTION/
AUSING TO FOCUS

e the following prompts to introduce
theme for today's service. Depending
on your congregation size, you may
nt to ask them to consider the following
estions in small groups and then
d back.

ere's quite a lot of detail in the Easter
ry. It's an important story. Today we're
ng to think about the story in a different
y. Let's start with a few questions:

at different parts of the story do you
ow? How do you remember it all?
n to someone near you and ask them
v they remember it. What helps them?

er 2 minutes, ask for feedback from the
ngregation as a whole, or from small
ups. Answers might include: repetition,
ers sharing part of the story, learning
r many years, a special book, reading
Bible regularly, going to church.

plain that today we are going to explore
elicious and colourful way of helping us
all key events in the Easter story.

2

GREEN

Our first colour is green.

*Lay the green fabric or flag over the altar,
or show the green segment of card or the
green segment on screen.*

This is to remind us of when Jesus rode
into Jerusalem astride a donkey. Let's
remember now.

Read together Matthew 21:1–11.

Sing together a song of praise, eg
'Hosanna'. As you sing, think about how
your life praises God.

After the song, explain to everyone that
different colours are going to help us
remember the order of the story. Each
colour will remind us of a specific element
of the story.

Green is for the palms of praise.

3

ORANGE

Our second colour is orange.

*Lay the orange fabric or flag over the altar
or show the orange segment of card or the
orange segment on screen.*

This is to remind us of how the mood of
the people around Jesus very quickly
changed from praise to betrayal and
arrest. Jesus met with his disciples, sharing
the bread and wine to remember the
Passover festival. Later, in the Garden of
Gethsemane, as Jesus prayed and the
disciples slept, Judas led a large crowd,
armed with swords and clubs, to arrest
Jesus, betrayed by Judas' kiss. Let's
remember now.

Read together Matthew 26:14–56.

Sing together a song that reflects this part
of the story, eg 'In the garden' by Michael
Card. As you sing, think about a time you
have let Jesus down.

'Orange for the swords ablaze.'

4

PURPLE

Purple is our third colour.

Lay the purple fabric or flag over the altar or show the purple segment of card or the purple segment on screen.

Purple is the traditional colour of royalty. This is to remind us of the fact that Jesus is King of all, and of how the soldiers and authorities mocked and humiliated him as he stood before the priests, Pilate the governor and Herod. Let's remember now.

Read together Matthew 27:11–31 and Luke 22:63 – 23:25.

After reading together, allow some quiet time for everyone to consider the following question:
'How do you make Jesus King of your life?'

'Purple for the royal robes.'

5

RED

Our fourth colour is red.

Lay the red fabric or flag over the altar or show the red segment of card or the red segment on screen.

This is to remind us of the painful death that Jesus went through; how he was forced to carry the cross to the hill of Golgotha; how two thieves were crucified with him, one of whom came to know God on the cross and join Jesus in heaven. Let's remember now.

Read together Luke 23:26–40.

After reading together, allow some quiet time for everyone to consider the following question:
'What does this tell us about how much Jesus loves us?'

'Red for the death he chose.'

6

BROWN

Brown is our fifth colour.

Lay the brown fabric or flag over the altar or show the brown segment of card or the brown segment on screen.

This is to remind us of why Jesus died. All of us do wrong things which get in the way of us being friends with God. Jesus did nothing wrong. His life was perfect. God gave his only Son to defeat sin, as a sacrifice for all our wrongdoing, so that each of us could be friends with God. Let's remember now.

Read together John 3:16.

Pray together. Invite the congregation to say sorry for their sin.

Invite everyone to think of something that they would like to say sorry to God for. You might say something like: 'Carrying wrong things in our hearts can make us feel sad, guilty and weighed down. Wrong thoughts and actions can hurt us or other people. Let's say sorry to God right now so that we can be put right with him.'

'Brown, the colour of our sin.'

7

LUE

ur sixth colour is blue.

*y the blue fabric or flag over the altar or
ow the blue segment of card or the blue
egment on screen.*

his is to remind us that it is through the
eath of Jesus that we are completely
rgiven and that each time, when we
ome before God to say sorry, we have
e chance of a new start. Let's remember
ow.

ead together 1 John 1:5–9.

ter reading, make some time to pray.
ou may wish to lead the congregation in a
ne of prayer, or choose a simple phrase
say together, such as: 'Thank you, Lord,
r dying for us on the cross to take away
ur sin.'

ng together a joyful song, giving thanks
r all that Jesus has done, eg 'Thank you,
sus' (Hillsong Worship).

lue for cleansing sin through him.'

8

YELLOW

Yellow is our seventh colour.

*Lay the yellow fabric or flag over the altar
or show the yellow segment of card or the
yellow segment on screen.*

This is to remind us of the glory of Jesus
when he rose from the dead. Let's
remember now.

Read together Luke 24:1–12 and John
20:10–23.

**'Yellow is the risen Christ Jesus
in glory.'**

9

PINK

Our final colour is pink.

*Lay the pink fabric or flag over the altar or
show the pink segment of card or the pink
segment on screen.*

'Pink for us to share the Easter story.'

This is to remind us that Jesus' friends were
so excited at learning that Jesus had risen
from the dead, that the first thing they did
was to rush to tell their friends. I wonder
how enthusiastic we are to share the good
news of the Easter story? Perhaps this is a
way we can this Easter:

Read out the whole of the Easter poem.

Green is for the palms of praise.
Orange for the swords ablaze.
Purple for the royal robes.
Red for the death he chose.
Brown, the colour of our sin.
Blue for cleansing sin through him.
Yellow, the risen Christ in glory.
Pink, we share the Easter story.

Sing together a closing song with an
Easter theme, eg 'Alive' (Hillsong *Young
and Free*).

After singing together, invite everyone to
come forward and collect some colourful
coated chocolates, with a copy of the
printed poem to take home.

HOW TO...
EXPLORE TOGETHER

Within our faith communities there is a rich diversity of God's people all at different stages in their faith development and spiritual experience, and all with different learning needs and preferences. We are a beautiful collection of artists, scholars, reflectors, dancers, data collectors, fact finders, readers, sculptors, writers, musicians, actors, talkers and listeners.

Explore Together places the Bible at the centre of this diversity. It is a new and practical tool for helping people to explore God's Word and hear his voice in a way that embraces their natural preferences. At the heart of Explore Together is a desire to see people hear from God and learn more of his love for them. It works with big groups, small groups, mixed-age groups, single-age groups, older people, young people, children, families, house groups, church congregations, youth groups, school groups… in fact, Explore Together can be used in any environment with any group dynamic.

THE SIX STEPS

There are six essential steps to an Explore Together session, each of which can be tailored to slot into any existing structure and space:

Preparation
Presenting the Bible
Prayer
Exploring
Sharing
Giving thanks

Step four provides an opportunity for people to engage with God's Word using the Explore Together questions and the six Explore Together zones. Each zone has been carefully designed to cater for particular learning needs and preferences:

Colour Zone
for those who learn by seeing
Listening Zone
for those who learn by hearing
Chat Zone
for those who learn by thinking aloud
Word Zone
for those who learn by reading
Busy Zone
for those who learn by doing
Quiet Zone
for those who learn by reflecting

Individuals can choose to spend all of their exploring time in one zone, but may also choose to visit several zones, depending on their preferences. There is no right or wrong amount of time to spend in a zone.

It is quite deliberate that no specific instructions are provided for each zone. Individuals are free to engage however they like with the resources provided in each area as they consider the Explore Together questions for the session.

If you'd like to know more about the ideas that underpin Explore Together and hear about our experiences of Explore Together in action please read our companion book:

Explore Together: The Journey

FREQUENTLY ASKED QUESTIONS

Our church has many people/a few people. Will Explore Together work here?

Over the last five years we have seen Explore Together used in small groups with only a few individuals but also in larger settings. We have known Explore Together to be used within a family home, but also within a programme at Spring Harvest for 450 children.

Key to the smooth running of Explore Together is preparation and planning. It is important to consider how the participants will arrange themselves into small groups. There is a danger that individuals who are close friends, or of similar age and background, will organise themselves into groups, therefore missing out on the excellent opportunity to learn from those who are a different age or stage in their lives. Inclusivity is key if individuals want to be challenged to learn something new.

While the planning, organisation and setting up of the zones are essential, large or small numbers of people do not present a challenge. No matter how large the group is, Step 5: Sharing is always done in small groups of three to five people. When feeding back in larger churches or groups, having a group of people with roving radio microphones in the congregation works very well.

Isn't Explore Together a bit chaotic, especially with children present?

It is chaotic in the sense that everyone is engaging in different ways, but not because the children are present. The explore zones are designed to embrace a range of learning preferences. Individuals of all ages very quickly find their own preferred activity and become occupied. Although there might be a buzz in the room, activity will be purposeful, colourful and appealing, and everyone has the freedom to move around and make choices in a safe and supportive environment. Many adults find the kinaesthetic dimension of Explore Together appealing too!

Does Explore Together need a lot of space? We have fixed pews in our church building that often restrict what we can do.

Explore Together can be planned carefully to fit flexibly into spaces that are different in size and organised in different ways. The explore zones do not all need to happen in one room, they could be spread out to happen in different areas. Your choice of activities can also be tailored to the amount of space you have, and you can creatively use the edges and corners of a room that contains pews. The smallest setting for Explore Together that we have heard about is at a dining room table in a family home.

What if someone says something completely off-the-wall?

My immediate response to this question is, 'it's better out than in'. What better place is there to explore your faith and ask your questions than in a community of faith – a community made up of many people with varying levels of understanding, wisdom, knowledge and experience? Explore Together provides a safe environment for people to express their thoughts and ideas, some of which may otherwise never be aired or challenged. The questions help to provide safe boundaries and keep the focus on the desirable aims and outcomes.

Good Friday
John 19:1–30

Themes: Good Friday, suffering, crucifixion, sacrifice, death, sorrow, God's love, forgiveness, the cross

This session is designed to help your community explore the events of Good Friday in a way that is meaningful to them. It can be used indoors or outdoors (with a little adaptation), and with people of all ages and stages of faith.

Prepare

Resources required
- 'Jesus dies' story text (from *The Big Bible Storybook*)
- 'Jesus dies' audio recording (from *The Big Bible Storybook* audio book)
- 'Good Friday' monologue
- 'Good Friday' image collection
- 'Good Friday' word collection
- John 19:1–30 (CEV)
- 'Good Friday' Explore Together questions (PDF and PowerPoint)

All available from www.exploretogether.org.

You will also need to gather:
- hot cross buns
- black paper, coloured pastels, white chalk, a roll of white paper, black marker pens
- audio versions of different translations of John 19:1–30
- lined notebooks, sticky notes, pens, pencils, paper
- biblical commentaries relating to John 19:1–30
- children's Bibles and Bible story books containing a version of John 19:1–30
- modelling clay, building blocks
- someone to deliver a Good Friday themed talk

Presenting the Bible

With the community gathered together, begin by sharing the words from John 19:1–30. Consider carefully which version of the Bible you choose to read from.

Without being tempted to answer them, introduce the following questions to your community for them to consider:

- **How do you feel about what happened to Jesus?**
- **What would you like to say to Jesus today?**
- **How does it feel to know that Jesus died for you?**
- **What does God's love mean to you?**

Pray

Pray for and with your community, asking God to help you hear from him. This time of prayer can be creative, interactive, responsive, meditative or sung. It could also include communion and intercession. Ensure that there is a place set aside where people can go if they feel that they need someone to pray with them specifically. Have a small team of people available to offer prayer if required. Prayer ministry should be available throughout an Explore Together session.

Explore

Read out your questions from Step 2 again or display them on a screen. Remind your community to consider these questions as they separate into their explore zones. Some may choose to consider all the questions while others may focus on just one. Some may completely ignore the questions and just open themselves up to God.

Invite your community to separate into small groups, around the zone(s) of their preference. Explain that individuals are welcome to spend as much or as little time in each zone as they wish, engaging at whatever level they feel comfortable. Depending upon where your quiet zone is located, you may wish to provide directions and remind people not to disturb one another when using this space.

Colour Zone

- black paper
- coloured pastels
- white chalk
- roll of white paper
- black marker pens
- hot cross buns
- 'Good Friday' image collection
- copies of the 'Good Friday' ET questions

Listening Zone

- 'Jesus dies' audio recording (from *The Big Bible Storybook* audio book)
- audio versions of different translations of John 19:1–30
- hot cross buns
- copies of the 'Good Friday' ET questions
- you may wish to deliver a Good Friday themed talk in this zone

Chat Zone

- a separate area with chairs, cushions or beanbags
- a chat zone host who is willing to read the passage again and then lead a discussion around the questions
- hot cross buns
- copies of John 19:1–30 (CEV) or Bibles
- copies of the 'Good Friday' ET questions

Word Zone

- lined notebooks
- sticky notes
- copies of 'Good Friday' monologue
- pens, pencils, paper
- biblical commentaries relating to John 19:1–30
- 'Good Friday' word collection
- hot cross buns
- 'Jesus dies' story text
- other children's Bibles and Bible story books containing a version of John 19:1–30
- copies of John 19:1–30 (CEV) or Bibles
- copies of the 'Good Friday' ET questions

Busy Zone

- modelling clay
- building blocks
- hot cross buns
- copies of the 'Good Friday' ET questions

Quiet Zone

- a separate area where people can be alone with their thoughts and God
- 'Good Friday' image collection (optional)
- copies of John 19:1–30 (CEV) or Bibles
- copies of the 'Good Friday' ET questions

Share

As your time for exploring together draws to a close, invite your community to come back together into small groups of three to five. Suggest that they share their responses to the questions posed at the beginning.

Giving thanks

Invite the explorers to share their reflections with the wider community, drawing together their responses and noting any common themes that emerge. Conclude by reading John 19:1–30 again (from the same Bible version used earlier). Then lead your community in a prayer, thanking God for all that he has revealed through this story. Encourage your community to continue their conversations about this story as they leave, and to take with them any artwork/writings/thoughts from the session.

aster is a great opportunity to run events
hat can help your church reach out to your
ommunity. These two family fun-day outlines
ffer comprehensive plans for running an
door or outdoor community event with an
aster theme.

FAMILY FUN DAY
TO BE CONTINUED...

CONCEPT

This fun day centres around four characters from the Easter story who each retell their experiences. Each one shows that, from difficult beginnings, God is transforming and renewing them. They, and all who have faith in Jesus, are on a journey of transformation. They are people 'to be continued'.

Each activity starts with an 'actor' telling their story from a simple script provided, setting the scene. They then interact with a group activity, ideally staying in character throughout. If this is not possible, simply have someone read out the monologue with a picture representing their 'character' on a projector or printed out on sheets.

Depending upon how many people you expect to attend, you could run this family day in two different ways. Either have characters deliver their monologues in turn, and after each monologue the whole congregation participates in the activity together. Alternatively, and especially if your congregation is fairly large, you may wish to split them into four groups. Each group would then 'visit' each character in turn, who should be established with their activity in a different area of your building.

SET UP FOR THE DAY

Costumes

You could go for traditional clothing, but this needs to be done well. Alternatively, contemporary clothes which hint at the character would work well. Peter, a deep-sea fisherman; John, a younger guy in a hoodie; Mary, wearing blue clothing; Pilate, dressed in a suit or a uniform.

Mary will also need a small box to hold or to while she is speaking. Inside it, there should be two small, different pieces of wood, a chisel and a lock of hair.

Readings

After each monologue and activity, a short reading is suggested. You might like to read these yourself, or ask people in the congregation in advance to read these at the appropriate moment.

Activity resources
Peter: rods, string, magnets, paper, scissors, paper clips

Pilate: paper, skin-friendly paints, cover-up and wash-up materials

Mary: small boxes (one per person), paper, pens, scissors

John: two buckets, a few plastic cups with small holes in the bottom, easy access to water supply, a tarpaulin or other suitable sheet to protect the floor from water (or a space to do this activity outside)

PETER

Peter tells everyone about the time that he met Jesus by the sea, going on to describe what happened when he denied ever having known Jesus at all.

'It was a normal fishing day when I first met him – Jesus, that is. Nothing's been normal since. We've been surrounded by crowds, alone on a mountain top, in a storm at sea. I was there when he healed people, right in front of me! We have had good times and bad, but the most difficult moment was after he got arrested. I knew something was wrong the week before – he was talking even more than usual about everything that God wanted him to do. We had a meal together in the upper room. It was odd, though. Not like a normal Passover at all. And then he went out for a walk – like, late. We all went with him to the Mount of Olives. Full of people it was, sleeping out because of the Passover. So he found a quiet place and he seemed really agitated, really concerned looking. He went off to pray nearby and we all went to sleep. Anyway, as we all woke up, soldiers arrived and arrested him. To cut a long story short, we all ran away. I know it probably wasn't the best thing to do, but I followed him from a distance. I mean, he's not just my master, he's my friend. I didn't want anything bad to happen to him. Around the fire in the courtyard people started recognising me and saying that I knew him. Three times I told them that I didn't. Then the cockerel crowed, just like Jesus said it would. I realised I'd let him down, just like he said. I looked at him and he lifted up his eyes and looked at me… he had love in his eyes… I was just ashamed. Ah, but that's not the end of the story. It gets better – a lot better! But before that, let's do something together that reminds me of what I used to do for a job before I met Jesus.'

Using rods, string and magnets, Peter helps people to make rods to catch fish. As he is explaining what the activity will consist of, he reminds everyone that when he was a fisherman, he would've used nets, not rods.

He instructs everyone to make some paper fish, with paper clips on their noses. Then he introduces a competition to see who can catch the most fish.

Afterwards, Peter says:

'I know how to catch fish, and now we've all tried it. But Jesus asked me to go out and catch people! If you were there with me, what would you have done?'

Read Mark 14:66–72.

Pilate describes what happened when he met Jesus. He explains what happened when Jesus was brought to trial.

'It was a grotty little place, Palestine. I mean, I don't know what I had done to be sent there! I was just biding my time waiting to be moved on. My wife hated it. She preferred the excitement of a real Roman town or even Rome itself. Here, there was always rebellion and fighting breaking out – particularly at Passover. Anyway, they brought this man Jesus, to me. They said he was a troublemaker, but it was obvious he hadn't done anything wrong; they just wanted to get rid of him. I tried my best to dissuade them, giving them the opportunity to release him instead of a known villain.

Then my wife had one of her dreams. "Have nothing to do with him. It's given me an awful nightmare," she told me. I didn't know what to do.

When I finally heard that some people were calling him a king… well, I couldn't have that. If that got back to Caesar I'd never get out of this forsaken backwater. But then again, what had he really done wrong?

I let the people decide. They chose to release that terrible villain, so I had no choice but to order my soldiers to crucify this Jesus. I had no option. Really. Honestly, I didn't.'

Pilate encourages everyone to make some hand print paintings, preferably with an Easter theme. After everyone has finished, he invites them all to wash their hands.

As everyone starts to wash their hands, Pilate reflects on the decision that he made to allow Jesus to be punished:

'That's what I did, you know. I washed my hands of Jesus. I didn't want to it to be all my fault.'

Read Matthew 27:11–26.

Mary tells everyone about the birth of her son, Jesus, and she goes on to explain what it was like being with him at the end.

'Where do I start about my boy? I know every mum thinks their child is wonderful, but I think I can safely say… well, he actually was. Look, I have a box of memories. Let me show you what's in my box.

Here's a piece of wood. I know it doesn't look like much, but it's a tiny piece of the wooden manger I laid him in on his first night. Oh, and here's a lock of his hair. Oh yes… his first chisel. Ah… He was good at his dad's trade, ended up putting beams in houses in Capernaum, before starting his ministry.

Here's another piece of wood. This… this one's not so good.

Sometimes I would join Jesus and the disciples. Other times, I heard from others what he was doing and saying. I was shocked when John came and told me, "Mary, they're killing him." What mother wants to know her son is being taken away? But I did want to know. I wanted to be there at the end, just as I was at the beginning.

So I just took a splinter of wood from the cross we left to take him to the tomb. I don't know why it just seemed right. But don't be too sad – that's not the end of the story. It gets better, I promise.

Mary hands out a small box to everyone and invites them to make small items to put inside that remind them of the good things that have happened in their own lives. (You can buy small boxes from craft suppliers.) Have paper and pens available for people to write ideas and put them in their boxes.

Read Luke 2:11–19.

JOHN

John describes what happened when he went to see Jesus' tomb three days after he had been laid inside.

'Hi, you've come to me at last – it's awesome. I can't wait to tell you! Me and my older brother, James, have been with Jesus for the past three years. We were always getting into trouble. Jesus called us the 'sons of thunder' – used to make us laugh!

It's been an amazing three years, but Jesus' final week was a nightmare. I was there with Mary when Jesus was on the cross and when they put him in the tomb. I'm not sure I've ever felt worse.

Then, three days later, as the sun is rising, the women come running in, yelling, shouting and jumping, saying the stone in front of the tomb has been rolled away and Jesus isn't there. He isn't there? The stone has moved? I didn't know what to think!

Peter and I legged it to the tomb. I got there first and it was true, they were right – the stone had gone, and when I looked in the tomb, he wasn't there!

It was only later we realised that he was alive. But even that's not the end of the story…'

John explains that carrying messages can sometimes be hard work. That day, people had gone back and forth to Jesus' tomb, carrying an incredible message – Jesus wasn't dead, he was alive!

John then invites everyone to participate in a running game, carrying water from one bucket to another using a plastic cup with holes in. He says that the water to be carried back and forth is a bit like the messages that went back and forth on that morning.

It may work well to divide the group into teams, giving every team member a turn to carry some water, and then assessing which team has successfully delivered most of the 'message'!

Read John 20:3–8.

ROUND UP

Draw everyone back together and invite Peter, Pilate, Mary and John to stand with you at the front. Using the following words (or your own if you prefer), remind people of all that they have heard today from each character, and offer them some closing thoughts to consider before they depart.

I hope you've enjoyed meeting or thinking about these different characters from the Easter story. Let's think about everything they shared.

For Pilate, his story was over. He disappeared from history – perhaps his wife got the posting she wanted.

For Peter, it wasn't the end. He saw Jesus again when he went fishing. He jumped out of the boat to meet him. Jesus even cooked him breakfast on the beach. Peter went on to tell hundreds and thousands of people about everything that Jesus had done.

For Mary, there was more to her story, too. She'd been there right from the beginning when Jesus was born and she was still there when the Holy Spirit came at Pentecost and the church was born.

And John's part wasn't over either. John went on to be a leader in the early church. He had a really important part to play in how the church grew in its early days.

Peter, Mary and John were all 'to be continued' people. Jesus had met them and changed their lives, but he hadn't finished with them. Easter shows us that God has not finished with us either. He loves us and wants us to become the people he knows we can be. We are part of his kingdom, here in this place, at this time, as we celebrate Easter together.

FAMILY FUN DAY
A-L-I-V-E

CONCEPT

This fun day is based around each letter of the word 'ALIVE'. During each activity, one of the five letters is revealed and gradually spells the whole word. The journey aims to build familiarity with the Easter story for those who are new to church, as well as being thought-provoking for Christians more familiar with it. Adults and children will work together, and activities should promote discussion and thought for all. The end of the day rounds up with the word being revealed in full and gently expounded upon by a leader. Halfway through the day, perhaps after three of the activities, make time for a break for a shared lunch or picnic, then continue with the last two activities and end with the final round-up.

SET UP FOR THE DAY

The day is designed for any size of group but if you expect larger numbers it is best to use five separate areas, one for each activity. In each area you will need to place a response sheet, which encourages people to guess the letter the activity represents and how it belongs in the Easter story.

Don't make the order of the letters obvious – place activities as randomly as your space allows, making it a little harder to work out the word. You could create some large letters big enough to decorate with white fairy lights. Reveal the letters as they are discovered, or all at once during the round up session, for greater impact.

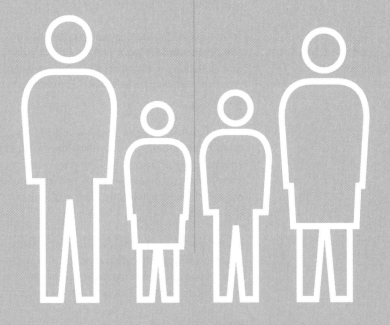

A IS FOR ART – MURAL OF THE ASTER STORY

is group activity provides opportunity to colour in the ster story as a large mural. also creates something to play in church afterwards other members of the ngregation to enjoy. Using ints (or pens), allow people colour in the huge picture wever they want to. You will ed to be aware of numbers decide if you need more an one painting or if all can rk together on the me mural.

eparing your mural
ere are a number of options this activity. The illustration have provided on page 95 uld ideally be copied onto ery large sheet of paper. e easiest way to do this curately is to fix your paper a wall, print the picture

onto an acetate, project the image using an old overhead projector, then draw over the projected outlines. A more skilled artist could do this freehand, using a grid system, or easiest of all you can buy a pre-printed mural sheet from www.eve2.co.uk.

Telling the story
As people of all ages join in with completing the mural, the person leading the activity can talk through the story. Try to refer to each part of the mural as you retell the Easter story, and remember that some people in your group may be hearing it for the very first time.

Question to think about
As people paint or draw, invite them to ask you any questions they may have about the Easter story. Don't feel that you need to be able to answer every question – rather, join in with their wondering.

L IS FOR LARGE OR LIFE-SIZED – MAKING A ROMAN SOLDIER

This activity is designed for all ages and is great fun, no matter how old you are! The aim is to create a Roman soldier. Groups can either dress someone up using various materials such as foil, cardboard and red fabric, to look like a soldier; or draw around someone laying down on a huge, life-sized sheet of paper and decorate the outline to look like a soldier, using paints/pens and various craft materials. When each group has made their soldier, take a photo and compare at the end to decide on a winner.

For more adventurous groups, you might choose to provide lots of Lego or other building bricks with which to make a soldier.

Preparing your soldiers
(Depending on which activity you use)
- Cardboard for a helmet, lots of tinfoil and red fabric
- A large sheet of paper, suitable collage items (foil, fabric, cardboard, etc), paints, pens
- Lots of lego or other suitable building bricks
- A picture of a centurion from the internet or a Bible encyclopedia as a helpful guide

Telling the story
While people are making their soldier, or perhaps after they have finished, a leader should share the parts of the Easter story involving Roman soldiers. For example:

After Jesus' trial, the roman governor, Pontius Pilate, handed him over to his soldiers to do what they were trained to do – kill or execute people. The Roman Empire stretched all the way from Spain to Egypt at that time, and the Romans chose to keep the peace by force. Roman soldiers were well trained, and obeyed their orders without question. But the Bible tells us that one soldier who saw Jesus die on the cross realised that something was different about this man. Just after Jesus died, the soldier said 'Jesus must really have been a good man!' (Luke 23:47, CEV).

Question to think about:
'Why do you think that was?'

Invite your group to talk through their responses to this question before they move on to the next activity.

I

I IS FOR INVENT – INVENT SOMETHING NEW

Each group should try to come up with an idea for a new invention, eg a household appliance, a new way of travelling, a new gadget, etc. This activity is intended to point to the resurrected Jesus as the first person of God's new creation.

Preparing your invention area

Set aside an area with chairs and other comfy seating. Provide paper, pens and a white board for writing up and developing ideas from each group.

Telling the story

When your groups have finished thinking about their new invention(s), ask them to find a comfy place to sit. Invite a leader to share the following story in their own words:

When Jesus met his disciples after he died, there was something new about him. He was real, but he seemed more real somehow. A NEW real. All the disciples recognised him, but they quickly realised he was different too. He could eat, walk and talk, but he could also do amazing things like appear in a room when all the doors were shut! This is because he was now very new. God had made him new again, and so the risen Jesus was the first part of God's new creation.

Question to think about:

'If Jesus is made new after he dies, do you think we can be, too?'

Invite your group to spend some time talking about their responses to this question.

V

V IS FOR VICTORY – GAMES TIME

This activity explores the idea of being victorious. If possible, you should aim for this activity to include a physical game. It could be as simple as a small scale football match or perhaps an indoor hockey tournament. If physical games are not appropriate for your groups or context, a variety of short board games could be played instead.

Preparing your games area

Depending upon how much time you have, you may want to have several game options available. Whatever type of game(s) you choose, make sure that everyone can participate. Consider the abilities and interests of those in your groups.

Make sure that everything needed for each game is prepared in advance. If you decide to include board games, make sure all the parts are present and in working order.

Telling the story

When the games are over and a winner has been declared, ask them how it feels to be victorious. Then invite a leader to talk about Jesus' victory, and how it holds significance for all of us:

When Jesus died he was put in a tomb. A great big stone was rolled over the entrance. Everyone who knew him was really sad – they thought they had lost him forever. But they hadn't. In fact, he came back in a new way – he had beaten death. He had won a great battle! A man in the Bible called Paul, wrote, 'Death has been swallowed up in victory' (1 Corinthians 15:54, NIV).

Question to think about:

'If Jesus has beaten death, what could that mean for us?'

Invite your group to split into pairs or groups of three and talk about their responses to this question.

IS FOR EGGS –
HOCOLATE FUN!

is is a classic Easter activity.
nvolves painting or piping
elted chocolate onto pre-
ught Easter eggs and adding
er edible decorations. Make
re that you consider issues
food hygiene and take into
count any allergies amongst
se in your groups.

en people arrive at this
tivity, they should all be
en a plain chocolate
g. Invite them to have fun
corating their egg with the
ocolate, edible icing, sweets,
inkles, etc provided.

tting up your Easter
g area

y some inexpensive hollow
ocolate eggs, enough for
ery person attending to
ve one each. Melt some
ocolate, white and dark
buy some ready-made
g in tubes) and get various
corative sprinkles or sweets.
ke sure you take into
count food hygiene issues
consider any allergies.
u are using melted
ocolate, you will also need to
vide clean brushes and/or
ing bags.

Telling the story

*As people decorate their eggs,
invite a leader to share this part
of the Easter story with them.
Depending on your group,
you may wish to wait until the
decorating time is over.*

Early in the morning, when the
women went to the tomb, they
got a bit of a shock. They were
expecting to get Jesus' body
ready to be buried, but when
they arrived, they found the
tomb was empty and Jesus
wasn't there! They went to
tell the other disciples who
couldn't believe what they
were hearing. They went to see
for themselves and they too
found the tomb empty. Jesus
had gone and the linen he was
wrapped in was left behind.
Just like the inside of our
Easter eggs today, the tomb
was empty!

Question to think about:

'Why don't you think the
disciples believed the women?'

Invite your group to spend
some time talking about their
responses to this question. If
appropriate, you might also like
to suggest they eat their eggs!

FINAL ROUND-UP

Draw everyone together and
spend a few minutes reviewing
all that has taken place. If
possible, bring your group
mural to the front, select a
winning group for the best
Roman soldier, share the best
new inventions and award
prizes to the winning teams
from the games area.

Telling the story

*Take a few moments to share
the Easter story in full. You
might like to use the following
words, or make up your own:*

Imagine the disciples walking
along a road to a town called
Emmaus, 20 miles away from
Jerusalem, three days after
Jesus had died. Just hours
after the news that Jesus' body
is missing, some people are
saying they have seen him,
alive. Are they completely
mad? What has happened?
What is going on?

The disciples are confused and
sad. They're arguing and their
argument is getting heated.
Then Jesus walks alongside
them. 'What's going on?' he
asks, 'What are you talking
about?'

They don't recognise him, they
don't see who he is. One of the
disciples turns to Jesus and
says, 'You're having a laugh,
aren't you? How can you not
know what has just happened
in the city?'

Then, the only person who
could tell them exactly what is
going on, asks them, 'What's
happened?'

So as they walk, they explain.
And then Jesus starts talking,
explaining what it all means,
explaining why the one they
call the Messiah had to die.

I suspect the journey doesn't
seem too long (no 'are we
nearly there yet?'), maybe their
feet seem lighter. They want to
hear more. They arrive at their
destination and they invite
Jesus to come in and stay with
them. They still haven't realised
who he is.

Just like the disciples, we
are all on a journey too. Life
is a journey, with its own ups
and downs every day. It can
sometimes take a dark, difficult
road for us to notice that there
is always someone walking
with us. He's a comforting
presence, not a shadowy
figure. When he starts
speaking, things just begin to
make sense. It's not always an
audible voice, sometimes it's
just a feeling.

The disciples invite Jesus
inside for a meal, and when
he sits down, they suddenly
recognise him. It's Jesus! It was
Jesus all along! 'Were not our
hearts burning within us while
he talked with us on the road?'
(Luke 24:32, NIV), they say.

He was right there with them
and he is right here with us. His
presence is with us now, here
in this place.

Take time to listen for his voice
this Easter. Jesus is not dead –
he is alive!

*If you haven't already, reveal
the letters from each activity,
remind people what each letter
represents and how it revealed
a part of the Easter story.*

EASTER STORY BOX

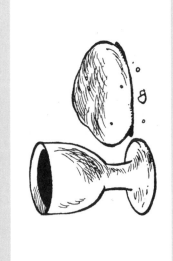

PRAYER POCKET

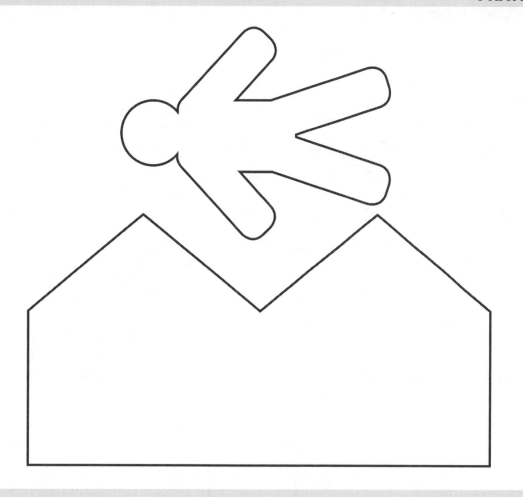

EASTER BEETLE

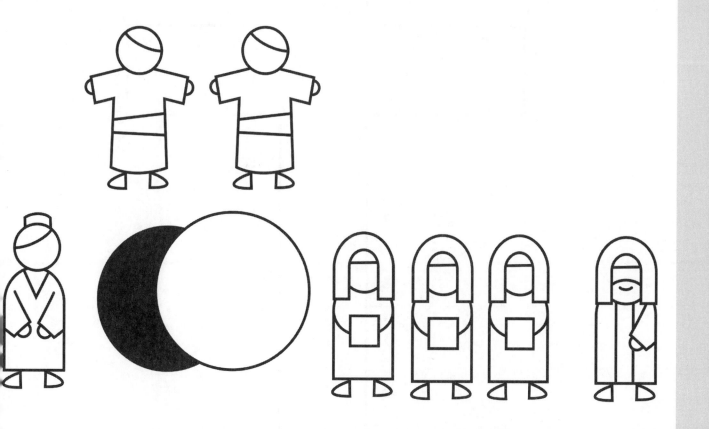

'JESUS IS RISEN' MAGNET

'JESUS IS RISEN' MAGNET

TORY OF EASTER BOARD GAME

START	1	2	Jesus enters Jerusalem to cheering crowds. Go forward three.	4	5	6	Jesus turns over the table in the Temple. Throw again.

							8

15	In Bethany, a woman pours expensive perfume on Jesus' head. Add 2 to next throw.	13	12	11	Jesus condemns the Pharisees. Go straight to Bethany.	The Pharisees try to trick Jesus. Go back 1.

16						

Jesus and his friends eat the Passover meal. Throw again.	Jesus says that someone will betray him. Go back 2.	19	20	Jesus shares bread and wine – his body and blood. Go forward 2.	22	23

						24

31	Jesus' friends run away. Follow their path.	29	28	Jesus is arrested – betrayed by a friend! Go back 3.	26	Jesus prays in a garden, but his friends can't stay awake. Miss a go.

Peter says he doesn't know Jesus. Miss a go.						

33	34	Jesus is put on trial. Wait until another player passes you.	36	37	38	Jesus is sentenced to death. Go back 2.

						40

47	46	Jesus is buried in a tomb. Swap places with the player at the back.	44	43	Jesus is put on a cross to die. Throw a 6 to move again.	41

48						

It's the Sabbath day and no one can do anything. Miss a go.	50	Jesus is alive! Go forward 3 spaces.	52	53	54	55	END (OR IS IT?)

TEMPLE IMAGE

ASTER MURAL

BREAKFAST LITURGY

Jesus, when we are carrying on with our ordinary lives
Come and join us for breakfast.

When we are overwhelmed by work
Interrupt our busyness with your rest and your peace.

When we think of you as distant and far from us
Join us at breakfast, the most casual meal of our day.

Come and make your company known to us
We want to begin each new day with you.

Jesus, meet us over our egg and soldiers

Or our Weetabix or porridge.

Your presence more precious

Than tea, coffee or our five-a-day!

Help us remember that though we might be tired,

Our hair and our teeth unbrushed,

You are there with us.

Our companion for each new day.

Jesus, you surprised the disciples with your company

when they weren't expecting you

and invited them to breakfast on the beach.

Each day, would you pop up in the

unexpected places in our lives.

Would you invite us to sit and eat with you.

Would you change our day

as we remember that you are here with us, always.

Amen.

EASTER POEM

Green is for the palms of praise.
Orange for the swords ablaze.
Purple for the royal robes.
Red for the death he chose.
Brown, the colour of our sin.
Blue for cleansing sin through him.
Yellow, the risen Christ in glory.
Pink, we share the Easter story.

EASTER POEM

Green is for the palms of praise.
Orange for the swords ablaze.
Purple for the royal robes.
Red for the death he chose.
Brown, the colour of our sin.
Blue for cleansing sin through him.
Yellow, the risen Christ in glory.
Pink, we share the Easter story.

EASTER POEM

Green is for the palms of praise.
Orange for the swords ablaze.
Purple for the royal robes.
Red for the death he chose.
Brown, the colour of our sin.
Blue for cleansing sin through him.
Yellow, the risen Christ in glory.
Pink, we share the Easter story.